MAKE FRIENDS WITH YOUR
HOUSE PLANTS
JERRY BAKER

Designed and Edited by Charles Cook

Simon and Schuster   New York

We would like to thank the following individuals and organizations for providing the photographs which appear in this book:
Cook—8, 12, 16, 20, 26, 42, 83; Oregon Bulb Farms—72; Roche—71; Wilkinson—6, 12, 15, 22, 23, 24, 32, 33, 39, 41, 43, 58, 59, 62, 69, 70, 84, 85, 86, 88, 90, 91.

SBN 671-21654-6 Paperback
Library of Congress Catalog Card Number: 73-8219
Designed by Charles Cook
Manufactured in the United States of America

2   3   4   5   6   7   8   9   10

Cover photo by Geo. W. Park Seed Co., Inc.

Contents

House Guests

The best reason for growing plants indoors is an extremely simple one—you like them. To be successful at anything, you must always start from this point. If you enjoy, admire and feel comforted by your plant friends, it is quite likely that they will feel the same way about you.

Some of us are just naturally gardeners. We enjoy gardening so much during the outdoor growing season that we feel lonesome without green and growing things around us during the colder months. We enjoy their beauty, but are also comforted by their cheerful presence—even on a cold winter day, there is a promise of spring to be felt just by a glance in their direction.

I really take pleasure in the feeling that my house plants are dependent upon me for care and comfort. Weeding, watering, feeding and giving them that occasional quarter turn to the light gives me something to look forward to every day—a bright few minutes of interest and fun. And of course there are other reasons—it is possible to reflect the entire color scheme of a room or to pick up the accent color by careful selection of the right plants.

Once people grew smaller plants than they do now—those that would fit on the kitchen window sill or on a small table placed where it would receive a southern exposure. But larger plants with larger leaves have been increasing in popularity for some time because they are so much more compatible with contemporary interiors.

Of course, the small plants are still popular, for their delicate flowers and foliage look well in the period settings that many of us prefer. Actually some plants are so adaptable that they look well in any location, if they are well-placed and properly lighted.

New species and varieties are constantly being introduced, so go into the florist shop occasionally and browse around. You may see something new and different that is just exactly right for that spot you have in mind. Or you may decide that one of the older, more familiar plants should receive the invitation to share your home with you.

Mother Nature
Is a City Slicker

If you're an apartment dweller, you've probably found that growing house plants is the best way to enjoy the marvelous and healthy hobby of gardening. It provides you with a rare opportunity to come into contact with nature and the great outdoors—something a bit hard to achieve in a crowded city park. There is also the happy feeling that the plants are yours, to be touched, loved and cared for—not just looked at from a distance.

If you combine your little window garden with a bird feeder, you've brought a bit of country living into the city, which is all the more important if you have young children, for children love flowers as naturally as you do and are intensely interested in watching them develop new leaves or buds. They will be as delighted as you are when they begin to blossom.

Plants can add immeasurable joy to the lives of the elderly or the physically handicapped who have little strength for outdoor gardening. And members of the work-a-day world, who have only a few minutes each day to devote to gardening, will be happy to know there are easy-to-grow plants which give much but demand little.

Of course, there are all sorts of rules for success with house plants just as there are for vegetables, trees, roses or anything else you may want to grow, but real success is largely a state of mind. If you want to succeed, you will. Growing things is an inexact but fascinating science, and experimentation is all part of the fun. And fun it should be, for a light-hearted approach is the most necessary factor. By this I do not mean carelessness or neglect—far from it! I simply mean that you should enjoy what you are doing. If you don't, you have no business growing plants indoors at all. Get yourself a cat or a

dog or take up china painting!

People used to think that having plants in the house was unhealthy, that they used up the oxygen in the air or something. Just the opposite is true—plants filter out impurities in the air and make it cleaner. They not only provide us with beauty and pleasure, they improve our physical well being too.

Most of us have gotten soft. We tend to keep our homes too warm in the winter—several degrees warmer than is comfortable for most plants. Actually, most of us would be more comfortable in a cooler atmosphere and probably far less susceptible to the discomfort of colds and other winter inconveniences. And keeping cool can also be good for the pocketbook—especially if you remember to cut down the thermostat at night. Your plants enjoy a cooler temperature at that time, just as they do when growing in their natural habitat.

A continuous temperature of over 70 degrees usually results in your plants becoming leggy and much less resistant to insect pests and diseases. Even the flowers they produce will be of poorer quality. Of course it is difficult to reduce the daytime temperature more than a few degrees. If you drop the temperature in your house to refrigerator level for the sake of your plants, you'll soon begin to resent their presence. And, don't think they won't know it!

The best solution to this dilemma is a compromise. When you go to bed, cut the temperature to somewhere between 60 and 70 degrees, the closer to 60 the better. If this is not possible and your plants are in containers of a readily movable size, move them to a cool room during the night, then return them to their accustomed place during the day. They, too, will be rested and fresh after a good night's sleep and will show their appreciation in increased vitality and beauty.

A hostess cart (Grandma Putt would've called it a tea cart) can be very useful. Use it as your plant stand during the day, then wheel your plants into a cooler room at night. You can use a toy wagon to serve the same purpose.

HOUSE PLANTS PREFER A TEMP. CLOSER TO 60° THAN 70°!

60°

*If your plants don't get enough
sunlight, you may have to supply
artificial light.*

Lighting

Very few rooms permit enough light to balance the amount of heat. And light is a limiting factor in growing many house plants. Of course growing plants under fluorescent lights alleviates much of this problem.

Nearly all flowering plants do best if given full light, especially during the winter. Tropical foliage plants do better in reduced light.

When you grow indoor plants under

Tropical Temperament

Of course, temperature preferences vary from plant to plant, just as they do from person to person, so if you feel you must have all the rooms warm all the time, choose plants with similar tastes. You should get along well with the tropicals. African violets, for example, will grow well with a temperature of 65 to 70 degrees at night and the same during the day—or even 10 degrees higher.

If you prefer a cooler atmosphere, try making friends with hydrangea, cineraria, cyclamen or primroses for a start. These Eskimos prefer 65 to 75 degrees in the daytime and 55 to 60 degrees at night.

Don't let any of your plants get frostbitten from pressing their noses against a windowpane. Pull the curtains or venetian blinds on cold nights or place a layer of paper between the plants and the window. African violets are especially sensitive to this type of chilling experience.

Of course, the other extreme is just as bad. You don't want to burn their toes by placing them too near radiators or hot air vents. You know how indoor heating dries your skin. Well, it does the same for your plants' complexions.

8

"Bah humbug! We shady characters hate sunshine."

fluorescent lights, every day is a sunny day. You can have "windows" any place in the house, and it "rains" only when you want it to. There need be no seasonal adjustment, and you do not have to give your plants that quarter turn they must have when grown on the window sill.

Plants will grow and flower, even in the darkest city apartment. Growing under artificial light has given gardeners a whole new field of horticulture and made this pleasure possible to thousands who do not have space for an outdoor garden.

Experiments have shown that the length of time plants are lighted is more important than the intensity of light. All plants grow much more sturdily with increased intensity—but only up to a certain point. Plants can be divided into four classifications according to the amount of exposure they require. The classifications are: (1) the long-day plants (2) the short-day plants (3) those that are indifferent to the length of daylight (4) those that need an intermediate day length. Some characteristics of plant growth, such as runner production in strawberries and bulbing in onions, require a long day, while tuber formation in tuberous begonias requires a short day. The height of many plants may also be limited or extended by varying the day length.

Summer-blooming plants obviously need a long period of daylight, about fourteen hours. If you provide artificial light, they will blossom during the winter too.

The short-day plant needs only about ten hours of daylight. By putting chrysanthemums in the dark in the afternoon, you can force early blossoms in summer. This is also the reason that they sometimes start budding during long periods of very cloudy weather. The reason that many poinsettias fail to blossom a second year is because they are growing in your living room with light on them through the evening. Set them in a dark room, but be sure the temperature is not less than 60 degrees at night. Study the natural preferences of your plants so you can provide for their needs.

"I don't mind growing under artificial light—as long as it's a spotlight."

Shed Some Light on the Subject

Plants grown in the average house receive, even when next to a window, considerably less light than when outside. Now that plants are being so widely used as a part of the interior decoration, they are often placed in the darkest part of the room so that they may add life and light to that particular spot. These plants, even though they may be chosen from varieties which require less light than the average flowering house plant, will

"I don't mind growing under artificial light—as long as it's a spotlight."

have improved growth and appearance if some provision is made to give them more light. Placing them in a sunny window or under lights for as little as four to six hours a day should help.

For most indoor gardening, fluorescent light bulbs are more satisfactory than ordinary filament type. Fluorescent bulbs give off less heat and can therefore be placed closer to the plant. About a foot above the plants usually gives the best results. Regardless of the type of bulb, be sure to use a good reflector for directing the light where it will be of the most value.

Since the most important factors that govern a plant's growth—light, temperature, humidity, aeration and even nutrition—vary from one household to another, it is difficult to give hard and fast rules for cultivating plants indoors under artificial light. Experiment and observe, developing your own rules adapted to your own conditions. Watch the plant's reactions; in its own way it will tell you if it is happy and content with conditions you are providing. If it isn't, be cautious about making any sudden changes. Plants, like people, are often shocked when subjected to sudden intensities of light, heat or cold. Whatever change you decide to make, do it gradually. Reactions to adverse conditions are more quickly noticeable and once they occur, they take a long time to overcome. Try not to let this happen.

For greatest success, a nice balance should be maintained between the various growth factors. For instance, plants growing in decreased light need a lower temperature and less water than those growing in strong light.

Remember also that a plant can use the available food only when there is sufficient light for it to carry on the process of photosynthesis. Additional light results in a shorter, stockier plant, while too little light causes plants to become "leggy" and weak.

If your plants are not growing well in their present location, check the light before you force more food on them and give them indigestion.

Watering

Moisture in the atmosphere will be as good for you as it is for your plants. You don't have to believe me—just check the counter where the beauty perparations are sold. Count the number of "moisturizer" creams and lotions that are being offered and look at the prices. If this isn't enough to convince you to do something about the dry air in your home, think of your plants. Did you see a moisturizer for Phyllis Philodendron? Of course not! So what do you do to protect her (and yourself) from dry, wrinkled skin?

A moist atmosphere is admittedly difficult to maintain in a modern heated home. Plants tend to dry out gradually, and as this happens, they become unhealthy and much more susceptible to insects and diseases. With some plants this condition can be overcome by spraying the foliage once a day. This does not, however, apply to African violets.

You might also set your pots in a galvanized pan filled with pebbles and water. If you water plants this way, the evaporation of the surplus water from among the pebbles will keep the humidity higher. And if the pots are unglazed clay they will absorb some of the moisture from the pebbles as well.

Plants do well in the kitchen where steam from cooking and dishwashing keeps the air humid.

Set a pan of water on the radiator and allow it to evaporate. Or, on days when you notice that the air is especially dry, set a large pan of water on the stove and let it boil. Grandma Putt always managed to squeeze all her favorite houseplants into the kitchen for the winter. It was all very cozy, and the steam from cooking and dishwashing made the plants glow with health.

But the best way to be really sure that both you and your plants are receiving the correct amount of moisture is to buy and use a mechanical humidifier. This is generally not an expensive device and it will benefit you as much as your plants.

It is also very important to keep the soil moist so plants will produce a good root system and be able to replace the water they lose through the leaves. This is particularly important in winter.

All water may look alike, but it's not. Some is good for your plants; some is not. Rain water or melted snow is the most desirable but not always available. Using distilled water is a good idea too, especially if your tap water contains a high concentration of fluoride and other soluble salts. (Since plants don't have teeth, they don't need fluoride.) When you defrost your refrigerator, save the water that collects. It's purer than tap water and your plants will love it.

12

If you must use tap water, place a layer of agricultural charcoal over the top of the soil to filter any additives. And do remember to use room-temperature water. In the winter, water from the faucet may be much colder than you realize, so be considerate. Your plants don't like a cold splash any more than you do.

For most plants, it really doesn't matter whether you pour on water from the top or allow it to rise from a saucer through a hole in the bottom of the pot. As a matter of fact, changing the procedure is sometimes a good idea. It insures that the whole soil mass becomes wet and prevents the formation of soluble salt deposits on the surface.

Pots with an automatic watering wick in the bottom are perfect for people who don't have a lot of time to devote to their house plants and for people going on vacations. Just be sure to check occasionally and to add water to the surface of the soil at least once or twice a month.

Don't Drown Plants in Love

Never allow your plants to get more than a little thirsty. If you wait to water them until the soil is as parched and dry as a desert, they'll wilt and the stems will eventually

"I said I was thirsty, but this is getting ridiculous!"

become hard and woody. If, on the other hand, you turn your flower pots into mini-swamps, your plants will drown. When the cavities between the soil particles are filled with water instead of oxygen for long periods of time, the roots become oxygen starved and eventually decay. When this happens, you'll become painfully aware that your pampered plant is in serious trouble.

You don't give your children a steady diet of double chocolate malted milk shakes just because they like them, do you? Of course not! You don't want them wearing dentures at the age of twelve. Use the same good judgment with your house plants. Don't overwater them!

To avoid making holes in the soil and exposing roots, place a small flat stone on top of the soil in each pot and slowly pour the water over this.

You'll learn how much water each of your plants needs as you get to know them better. Cacti, for example, need very little water and will quickly rot if you keep their feet wet.

Here are a few hints to help you avoid house plant tragedies until you become more experienced.

Check your plants every day. Never allow them to wilt.

When watering is necessary, do so thoroughly, then allow all the excess to drain away. The best time to do this is early morning.

If daily watering doesn't seem to be sufficient, you may need to repot the plant, leaving space in the top for water.

If the air in your house is very dry, frequent, heavy watering may be necessary to compensate for the evaporation of water from leaf surfaces.

Slow-growing plants, like mother-in-law tongues and Christmas cacti, need far less water than rapid-growing plants, like ferns, fuchsias, begonias and palms. Easy-care geraniums are quite happy with one good soaking a week.

One of the best investments you can make is an inexpensive one—a sprayer, which can be used for watering fragile plants or "mist-

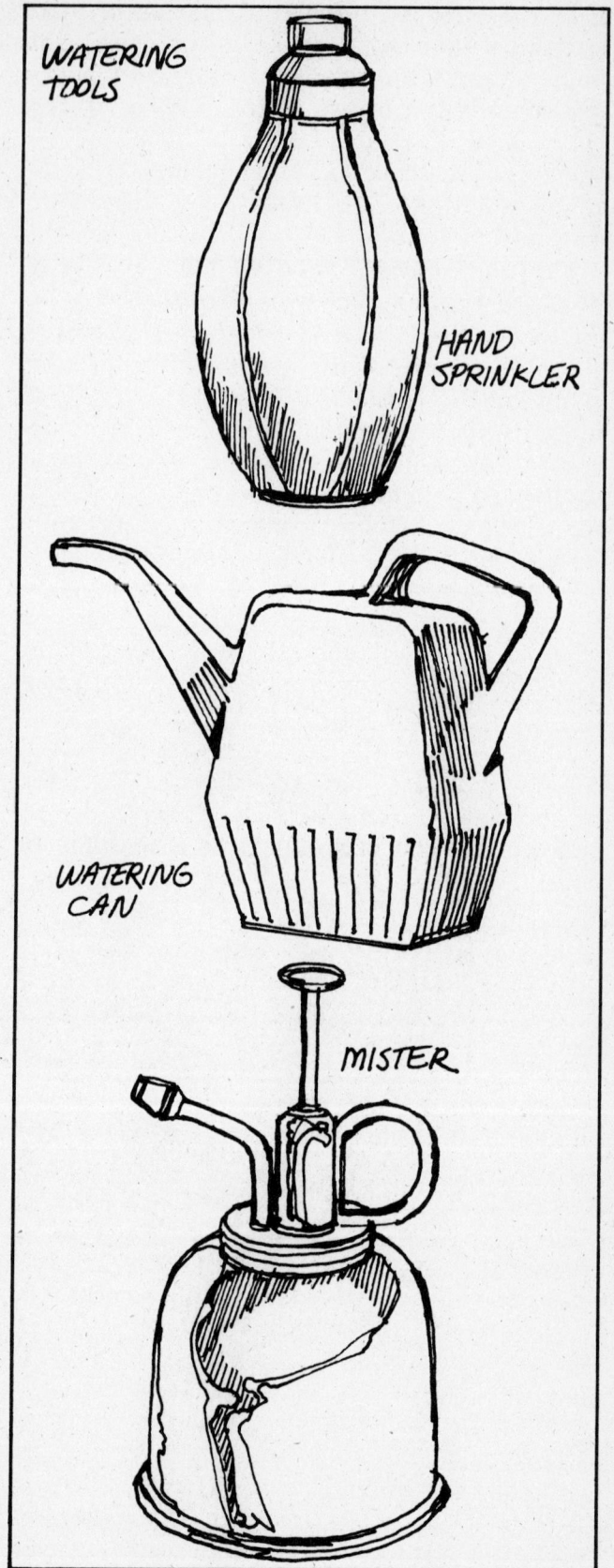

WATERING TOOLS

HAND SPRINKLER

WATERING CAN

MISTER

ing" pesticides. Most plants enjoy an occasional light spray.

The Two-Week Tragedy

That two week's vacation need not be a period of agony either for you or your plants. Getting someone to look in on the plants while you are gone is the best answer—arrange a trade with a gardener friend.

If you cannot get someone to care for your plants, cover them with a large polyethylene sheet and tie it to the pot or box to prevent loss of moisture. If possible, reduce the lighting to eight hours a day. If you have time before leaving, you can train the plants to get along with less water—many will adjust better than you think. If not, just give them a good drink before you leave.

Plants cared for like this can get along satisfactorily by themselves for about two weeks. If you must be away for more than two weeks, you can expect to lose some of your plants, especially the flowering ones.

Cross-Country Travelers

Many cherished house plants came across this country with their owners in covered wagons. Today it takes less time to move but you still have to plan in advance for the comfort of your plants. If you do, there is no reason why they should not arrive in good condition. Secure a sturdy cardboard box, large enough to set the pots in and tall enough so they will not have their tops broken. If the trip will take several days, water them well and put a large plastic bag over each pot. Roll up the excess and make a sort of collar around the pot. Stuff additional bags in between the pots so they won't rock around or turn over.

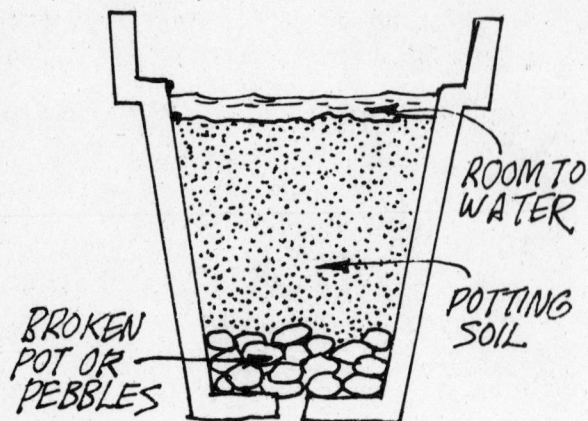

BROKEN POT OR PEBBLES

ROOM TO WATER

POTTING SOIL

temperature, then spray with a weak solution of tea. This will act as a rubdown or antiseptic.

This wash will keep the bugs away, and a pinch of ant powder added to the soil will kill any bugs already there. Don't ever use any leaf polish. Plants breathe through their leaves, so don't plug their little noses.

Automatic watering pots are available and consist of a pot with a glass wick, which hangs in a reservoir of water. The wick enables the water from the reservoir to moisten the soil. This method is an excellent choice for many plants, especially African violets. It is also good for starting seed.

Are Your Plants Crocked?

If you have been properly watering your plants and they still seem to be too moist, check to be sure the drainage vents are not clogged. If you do not repot a newly purchased plant, you may not notice that there is no crocking in the bottom for drainage. If this is the case, or if the pot has insufficient drainage, remove the plant and clean out the pot. Put in pieces of a broken clay pot or pebbles or bits of broken brick. If the plant has not grown too large, put it back into the same pot, then water, if necessary, and check to see if it is draining properly.

You can make many of your plants happy by giving them a steam bath once or twice a month. Place a brick or wooden block in the middle of a large bucket and set the plant on it, then add steaming water to the bottom of the container. Do not let the water touch the pot or the plant. Let the plant enjoy its improvised sauna for five or six minutes, then return it to its favorite spot—refreshed and happy.

Clean plants are naturally happy, so wash them twice a month with good old soap and water. Use two tablespoons of mild liquid soap in a half-gallon of room temperature water. Rinse with water of the same

Choosing

House plants can be a tonic for body and mind—cheering you up on those days when the rest of your world seems devoid of sunshine. If your fingers are stiffening with arthritis, plants can be therapeutic. Working in warm soil is as comforting as working with warm water. Making your plants comfortable will often do the same for you.

But plants have varying personalities. Before you invite them in as guests, eventually to become family members, there are some things you should consider.

Basically there are five types to choose from—foliage plants, flowering house plants, flowering pot plants, bulbs, and cacti and succulents. Foliage plants usually grow more slowly and change least of all. They are quite likely to become permanent residents.

Flowering house plants are also permanent. Choose your colors with care, so they will contrast or harmonize with the rest of the room.

Flowering pot plants and bulbs may be considered temporary visitors in the house. If you become especially fond of them, you may replant them outside if they are hardy plants like chrysanthemums. Some bulbs may also be saved to use again in an outdoor setting.

Cacti and many types of succulents are fun plants and often become collector's items. They have many forms and faces—have you ever seen an "old man" cactus with its wooly white hair near the top?

The fun of indoor gardening is in choosing the most suitable plants, so let's consider the ground rules.

1. Make sure the plants you select really appeal to you. Don't pick them because you saw them growing in the house of a friend, or because they're the latest fad.

2. Be sure they are suitable for your home climate. It's your home, remember. They will be the happiest, and so will you, if you both enjoy the same type of environment.

3. Be sure they are no more difficult to grow than the time and experience you have to offer. If you are a beginning gardener, you have a choice of many easy and inexpensive plants. There will be no great loss (except possibly an emotional one) if they do not do well or die.

Consult your local florist about this. In all likelihood, he sells more philodendrons than any other house plant. They are tolerant of the warm conditions found in most modern homes and they stand poor light better than almost any other house plant. They will grow better if placed in a well-lighted window from October till April, when the sun's rays are weaker.

Remember that house plants are raised in greenhouses where the air is warm and humid. They are not accustomed to the world outside. Try to buy from a reliable supplier who makes sure that the plants have been properly "hardened off" and will not be too disconcerted by the change in the environment.

You can buy house plants at any time of the year, but it is best to buy delicate varieties in spring or summer. Be sure the plant is sturdy, not spindly, has no damaged leaves and is free from insects.

If the weather is cold, wrap the plant well before leaving the nursery. Treat it gently for about a week after you bring it home, keeping it out of drafts and direct sunlight. Don't give it too much heat or water. If it continues to do well, place it in its permanent location and treat it normally.

Potting

Good soil mixes are a must for indoor gardening, but again you must understand the individual preferences of your plants. You can't just go out in your back yard and scoop up a shovelful of soil and expect your plants to thrive in it. Some might, but the odds aren't good.

For the apartment dweller who does not have a place to prepare potting soils, time to do the work or a good source for ingredients, it's a good idea to buy one of the commercially prepared mixes. Most of these materials are sterile, weed-free and prove reasonably acceptable. However, they do have some disadvantages. Generally the material is fine and powdery and tends to pack, giving little capacity to absorb or hold water. It lacks the springiness of natural compost and may, in time, close out the air.

If you must work with such a commercially prepared mix, try adding a half teaspoon of a complete plant food to a six-inch pot of soil. This supplies the necessary nutrients for a

ADD ½ TEASPOON FERTILIZER TO POT OF BOUGHT POTTING SOIL

MAKE YOUR OWN POTTING SOIL

2 PARTS GARDEN SOIL

ONE PART COMPOST

ONE PART SAND

time. A complete plant food contains a balanced ration of nitrogen, phosphorus and potassium, necessary for plant growth,

Generally plants purchased from a reliable source are already potted in a mixture which will not need additional fertilizer for some time. Later purchase a good house-plant fertilizer (in concentrated form) and use according to the directions. Such fertilizers are usually available as tablets, liquids and soluble dry fertilizers. No matter what the form, moisten the soil before feeding—never feed a dry plant!

If you are a gardener and can make your own compost, nothing really takes its place. If you have only a small area, you can make enough compost for your house plants in a small, neat enclosure or in large plastic garbage bags.

For a good all-purpose potting soil, mix together two parts garden soil, one part compost (or leaf mold) and one part sand. This suits plants such as geraniums, amaryllis, dracaenas, oxalis and palms. Plants that need a high humus content, such as African violets, begonias, philodendrons and azaleas, will do well in a mixture of equal parts sand, peat moss, garden soil and compost.

Cacti and succulents, plants of or near the desert, need a gritty, lean growing medium. Most prosper in a mixture of one part garden soil, one part sand, one-half part compost and one-half part crushed clay flowerpot or brick. To each half bushel of this mixture, add a cup of ground horticultural limestone and a cup of bonemeal.

Most orchids and bromeliads are classed as epiphytes and are cultivated in such mediums as osmunda fiber, unshredded sphagnum moss and chipped redwood bark.

If you have no good source of supply for sand, consider using horticultural perlite, which makes an excellent substitute. Vermiculite, in place of leaf mold or compost, will lighten and condition heavy, sticky soil and make it acceptable to plants which need well-aerated soil. And these inexpensive substitutes are already sterilized.

Fight Fungus

There are two ways to kill the fungus diseases and pests in the soil—by chemicals or by heat. I prefer heat. With chemicals there is the possibility that the soil is not completely permeated by the substance used and chemicals may leave an undesirable residue.

Heating the soil is more efficient and is simple to do. Heat the soil to 210 to 212 degrees F. This is just at, or below, the boiling point of water. Keep it there for 15 to 40 minutes, depending on the type of soil you are baking. If your soil is heavy, use a longer baking time to achieve satisfactory results. Thirty minutes is a good average time to figure on.

If all this sounds too complicated, place a small potato on a pie tin of soil and bake in a 250 degree oven until the potato is tender. By then the soil will be sterilized as well.

After the heat has reached a point between 205 and 210 degrees it should not go much higher. Plants will not grow in an overbaked soil unless untreated soil is mixed with it.

The favorable organisms necessary to soil fertility, as well as those of the disease organisms, are killed when the soil is overbaked. Accurate sterilization, however, is beneficial to the soil. It eliminates pests and diseases and, through its action on the soil substances, increases the actual fertility. Generally speaking, a sterilized soil needs less nitrogenous fertilizer than usual. After sterilizing your soil, be very careful not to contaminate it again.

Soil that is mixed to duplicate, as closely as possible, the natural enviroment of a house plant will make it easier to grow that plant. As you become more and more interested in your plants and begin to communicate with each one on an individual basis, you will become increasingly aware of their personal likes and dislikes, and you will get to know what sort of soil each prefers.

There are two reasons why most potted plants do not do as well in ordinary topsoil (loam) as they do when this is mixed with other materials. When plants are potted, the soil is usually packed down firmly. Frequent watering tends to make it even more compact. If the soil is not naturally porous, free passage of water and air is seriously impeded. The second reason is that the amount of soil available to the roots of a potted plant is necessarily limited, so it cannot expand its root system. Thus, when frequent watering causes the nutrients to leach out—which they do more rapidly than in an outdoor garden— the roots become starved. Both these problems can be counteracted, to a large extent, by the addition of compost which contains a large amount of decayed organic matter. If this is not available, use commercial humus, sedge peat, peat moss or other similar material. Just as with "homemade" compost, the amount you add depends on the character of the soil and the type of plant you intend to grow. Whether homemade or commercial, it is the fibrous organic matter which helps porosity, slows down leaching and, as it decays, supplies more nutrients.

Porosity is also helped by the addition of coarse sand, finely broken brick or coarse coal cinders. These should never be more than a fourth to a third (by bulk) of the finished mixture, however.

Fertilizers added to potting mixes may include small amounts of dried cow manure, bone meal and wood ashes, but these should be added cautiously in small amounts. Other additions, depending on the type of plant grown, are crushed limestone or lime and chopped charcoal. If you have very young plants, use less than you would for more mature ones.

A real house-plant fan can never have too many pots.

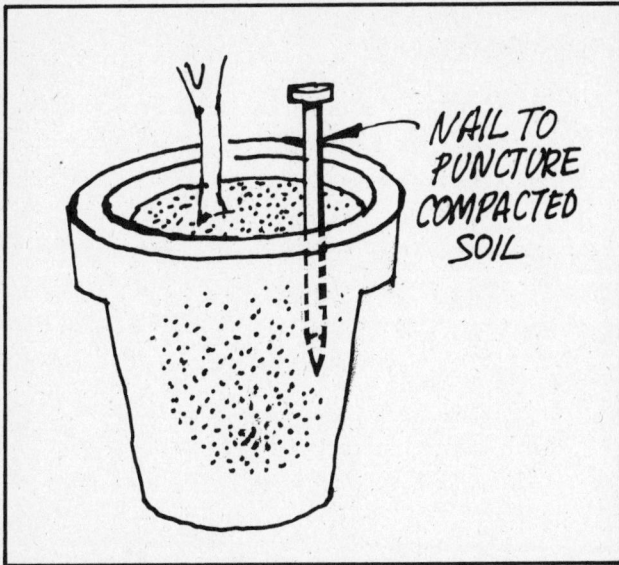

NAIL TO PUNCTURE COMPACTED SOIL

Acupuncture

Soil in good condition for plant growth should have about 50 percent solid (by volume) and 50 percent pore space. Sometimes soil, though not actually compacted, is so poorly drained that its pore spaces fill with water at the expense of air, and the plant roots in the area starve for oxygen.

As an emergency measure, you can perform acupuncture on plants suffering because of compacted or poorly drained soil. Take a long, slender nail and gently work it down into the soil. What you are doing is aerating the soil, so be careful not to stab the plant to death. The number of holes you need to make depends on the size of the pot. After the holes are made, water the plant.

This acupuncture treatment is not intended to cure the situation, only to give both you and the plant a "breather" until you find time to take care of the plant properly.

Lots of Pots

Potting can be a lot of fun! So don't start off with the idea that it's a back-breaking chore that must be gotten through somehow. Give some thought beforehand to your own personal comfort while you are doing this job.

It can even be a very pleasant, interesting and relaxing ritual. If you are miserable the plants will know, and they will feel your resentment. Your fingers will be clumsy when you handle them, and you might even break a few. So don't let this happen. I suggest building a special potting table or bench if you have room.

It makes sense to have your bench the right height, whether you prefer to work standing or sitting on a tall stool. You may enjoy a little soft music, so why not have a radio by your potting bench? A potting bench should also be sturdy. There will be times when it may have to hold a great deal of weight, so use lumber that is heavy enough to support it. Make sure that it does not wobble—few things are more frustrating than a potting bench that seems to be on its last legs. The bench should be large enough to hold all the items you will be using with plenty of room left for work space.

Another idea that will add to your convenience and speed clean-up operations is to have the top of your bench covered with a smooth-surfaced material, possibly formica. A shelf built above the back portion of the potting surface provides more storage space with no loss of work space. Place on this your flats, plants you have finished potting, or tools you are not using.

There are so many kinds and types of pots to choose from today that, to a beginner, it must seem bewildering. Clay pots are probably the oldest form and these, in small sizes, are most often used for "baby shoes," the first container into which seedlings are placed.

Clay pots are porous, and this is definitely an advantage. If the temperature is high, soil moisture evaporates through the pot walls which keeps the plant roots cooler. Also a clay pot is heavier than a plastic one and this extra weight stabilizes plants that tend to grow large or top-heavy. Clay pots are suitable for plants of almost any size as well as seedling plants.

Clay pots are easily broken (if you do accidently break one, save the shard for crocking) and, in time, they may get mossy unless specially treated. This green scum is a form of algae that grows on unused fertilizer and is a sign of overfeeding.

If you bought your plant already potted the natural tendency is to let it remain as is, until you suddenly realize something is wrong. First aid must be administered, but you aren't quite sure what this should be.

First, make sure the drainage vent isn't clogged. Even when pots have been well-crocked (pot shards, pebbles, or bits of brick placed over the drainage hole), loose soil sometimes works down between the crocks and, with continual watering, starts to pack.

Proper potting is the first step to house-plant success.

Sometimes the pot has not been crocked at all. To find out if it has been, take a pencil or a stick and poke around in the drainage hole. If it goes right through without hitting something hard, you may be reasonably sure that the pot has not been crocked. Remove the plant from the pot and start over. Turn the pot upside down and rap the rim on something hard. The plant, soil and all, will fall out into your hand.

Scrape some of the overwet soil from the bottom of the root ball and put it aside. Thoroughly clean the pot and delve into your box of broken shards. Overlap these over the drainage hole so the soil will not get down into it. Replace the plant and add as much new potting soil as may be necessary to bring it up to the correct height again.

Everything comes in Plastic

Plastic pots are inexpensive, lightweight, easily cleaned at repotting time and can be purchased in dozens of cheerful decorator colors.

If you're using a plastic pot, just remember that it's entirely different in its makeup from clay and takes different treatment. Cover the entire base of the pot with an inch or so of crocking material, then finish potting as usual. When you lift the filled pot, be sure to use both hands and hold it as nearly level as possible. If you grasp the edge of the pot with one hand, it may twist slightly and break as you lift it up.

Glazed pots will dress up your plants. They have the weight of a clay pot, combined with the color advantages of plastic. Be sure to check the bottom, for they come both with and without drainage holes. If you want to plant directly in the container, choose one with a drainage hole.

The other type of glazed pot—the one without the drainage hole—is often called a "jardiniere." It is really not a flower pot at all and should not be used for one. It is really a fancy holder for a plain-Jane clay or plastic pot.

Depending on the size of your jardiniere, place an inch or two of pebbles on the bottom before putting the pot inside. Also be sure that the dress-up pot is large enough. There should be 1 to 1½ inches of air space all around. Be cautious about watering, and check frequently to see that water is not rising in the container and drowning your plant.

Jardiniere

23

Wooden Shoes

I always fit my large plants with wooden shoes (tubs). If you are a do-it-yourself hobbyist you can make your own tubs and built-in planters. However, many attractive kinds are sold by mail and in local shops.

Palms, citrus trees, bay trees and many other large plants are becoming more and more popular as indoor accent pieces. If you have a large room or a greenhouse where a large plant will look well and have room to spread, you may want to consider growing it in a wooden tub. You may be forced to use one by an aggressive plant that is completely outgrowing its allotted space. Generally speaking, if your plant is large enough to require a container with a diameter of twelve inches or more, a wooden tub is often a better choice than a flowerpot of the same size.

The type of wood used for these tubs is very important. Florists often use inexpensive tubs of light construction, such as pine bound with wire. These are only intended to house a plant for a year or two and are not practical for the homeowner. Lifting and changing the home of a large tree or shrub is not something to be undertaken lightly, so plan to have it remain as long as possible in the first container you place it in.

Water-resistant woods of a heavy grade, such as redwood and cypress, last longer. They will not rot out as easily, are almost always constructed better, and are bound with stout steel bands or bolted together with steel rods.

If you do not like their color you can paint them. Paint the interior as well; just be sure you do this with a non-toxic paint. The inside may also be charred to increase resistance to decay. Do not, under any circumstances, paint the interior with creosote.

Large wooden tubs should never be set directly on the ground or floor. If they do not come equipped with legs, either make some or raise them off the floor with bricks or other supports. They must have this air space for proper drainage and to prevent the base of the tub from decaying.

Tubs made of redwood, cedar, cypress or fir are attractive without an outside finish and are resistant to decay.

Moving Up in Life

How can you tell when a plant is pot-bound? One of the signs of starvation and loss of vitality is shredding in the lower leaves. They turn brown or yellow and die. Plants are very tenacious. They will put all their vitality into the very tip end of each stem and will even sacrifice other leaves in order to do this. Never let your plants get that severely pot-bound, for those lower leaves will not grow again no matter what you do. The leaves of pot-bound plants often become progressively smaller in order to conserve nourishment. If the leaves on one of your plants seem to be shrinking, you'd better investigate.

Experience is still the best teacher. Don't be afraid to knock out a pot occasionally when your suspicions are aroused. Seldom is harm done by such an operation and if the plant is all right, simply replace it. The plant won't care—it might even enjoy the fun. You can be sure it will enjoy the attention and be glad you are solicitous of its comfort.

The first step in repotting is to make sure that you have on hand clean pots of a suitable size. If new clay pots are used, soak them in water for ten minutes or so and then let them dry before using.

Usually a clearance of ½ to 1½ inches between the ball of earth and the side of the new pot is about right. Make sure of adequate drainage by covering the hole on the bottom of the pot with a piece of broken flower pot, concave side downward. Add an inch or so of small clinkers or flowerpot chips. On top of this, place about half an inch of organic material, such as coarse compost, moss or flaky leafmold. This keeps the finer soil from sifting through and clogging the drain hole.

Remove the plant from its pot and rub off any loose surface soil. Disentangle the crocks of the plant if it has grown into them. This may damage the roots somewhat, but it must be done. Sometimes the roots have even grown through the drainage hole and

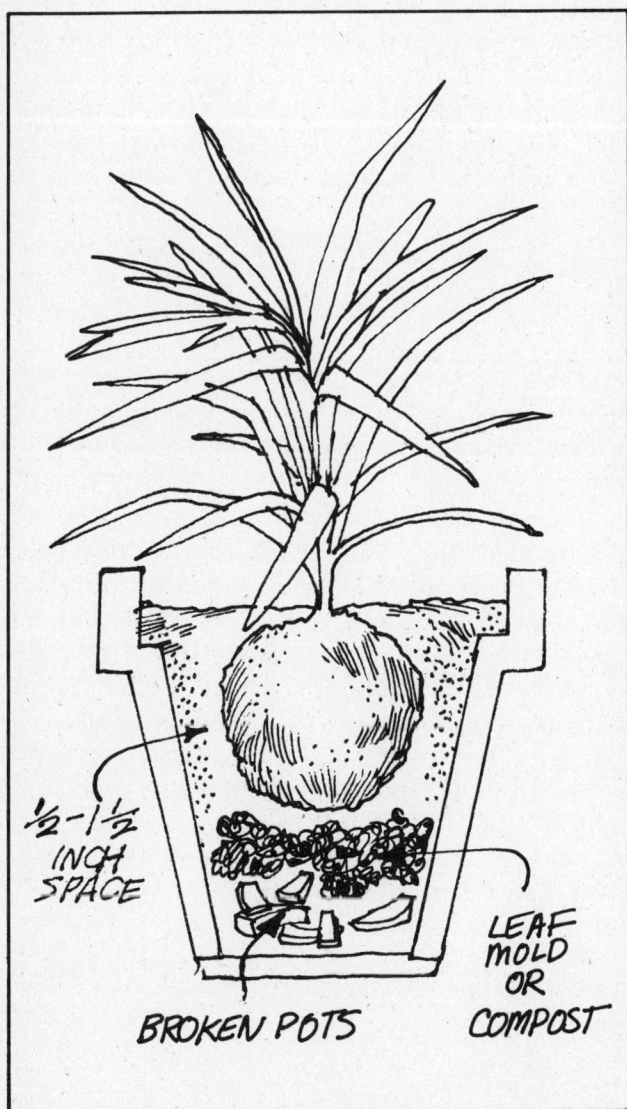

½-1½ INCH SPACE

BROKEN POTS

LEAF MOLD OR COMPOST

must be drawn back, which does still further damage. Just do the best you can.

Put enough soil in the new pot to bring the plant to the correct height. (The plant should be about an inch below the rim of the pot, depending on the pot size, so watering may be conveniently handled.)

Settle the soil by jarring the pot on the bench, then pack it down with your fingers to the same density as that of the old ball. Level the surface soil with your fingers.

Always keep in mind that the purpose of potting plants which are approaching maturity is to keep them in a healthy condition rather than to encourage continued growth. Most of us simply cannot go on re-potting plants indefinitely, for we will eventually run out of room.

A Summer Vacation

It is very difficult to draw a firm dividing line between house plants and outdoor plants—in many cases they are the same. Plants vary so much in their environmental needs that those that may safely winter over outdoors in one part of the country will freeze and die farther north. Sometimes house plants are placed outdoors when they outgrow the pots where they were originally grown.

Other plants, purchased while in bloom, may no longer be regarded with the same affection by their owners when they are spent. If such plants are reasonably hardy, as are chrysanthemums, they may be safely planted in the outdoor garden. If they prosper, they will make nice cut flowers for the house when blooming time comes round again.

Other plants, such as dwarf citrus trees, often renew their vigor and beauty if placed outdoors during the warm season of the year, but they must be brought in again when cooler weather approaches.

Some plants benefit by being sunk into the soil during the summer, right up to the pot rim. This may create a problem in the fall if the roots grow down through the hole into the garden soil. Nevertheless, this is something that many owners of house plants like to do.

An ideal spot for summering indoor plants outdoors is under a spreading shade tree, particularly if the tree is one that does not have heavy foliage or deep roots. Here the pots can be plunged into the soil to their full depth. They will receive the full benefit of refreshing summer showers and filtered sunlight.

Place your shade-loving plants on the northern side of the tree and dig a hole deep enough for them to sit in. If natural rainfall is not sufficient they must be watered. If necessary, spray for insect control. Give the pot a twist occasionally to keep the plant from rooting through the drainage hole.

In the fall, when temperatures begin to drop, lift out the pots, clean them off, and bring them back into the house. You may be agreeably surprised at how well they look after their summer vacation.

GRAFTING CACTI

Grafting different types of cacti together is remarkably easy, and the effects can be amusing or strikingly lovely. Some cacti grow more rapidly and bloom more readily when grafted onto a different understock than when growing on their own roots.

The common Christmas cactus, for example, grows much faster when it is grafted onto the Blue Candle cactus. Also, the graft will result in a graceful, weeping tree-shaped plant that will become especially beautiful when the Christmas cactus blooms.

To graft any two cacti together, first make a slit in the understock with an injector-razor blade. Take the scion (the piece of cactus you're going to insert into the understock) and use the razor blade to carefully taper the base of its stem. Insert the scion into the understock and pin it in place with a cactus thorn. Then put a rubber band around the understock. When the scion starts to grow in a few weeks, you'll know your graft was successful.

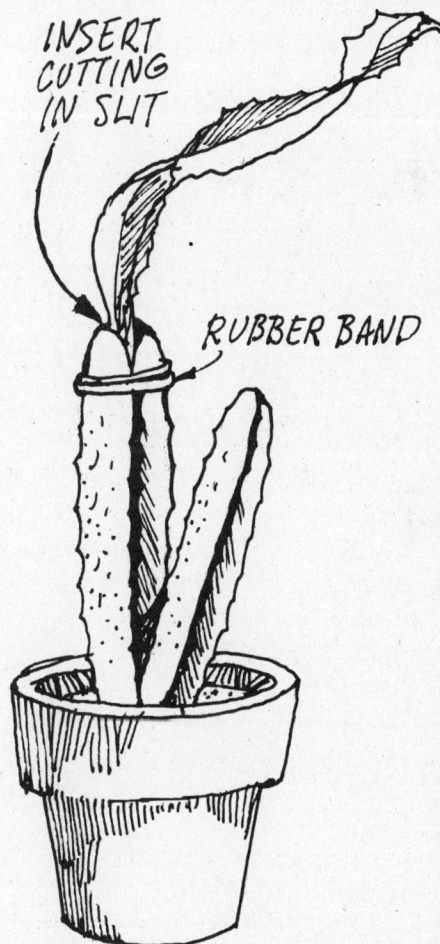

INSERT CUTTING IN SLIT

RUBBER BAND

Propagation

I like to have a lot of young plants on hand for several reasons. If one of the "regulars" in my collection starts to fade, I can quickly and easily replace him with a new star. Or I can fill my living room with a bevy of homegrown beauties if I like.

I guess I learned one of the best reasons for propagating plants from Grandma Putt. She always kept a few "slips" rooting on her kitchen window sill. Every time she pinched back her begonias, she'd stick the prunings in a glass of water or a pot of sand. After the slips had rooted, Grandma would pot them up and they'd gradually disappear, one by one. I wondered what happened to all those plants. She often took one or two with her when she went visiting—and she seldom came home empty-handed.

Don't be timid! If you think plant propagation is only for experts with all sorts of special equipment, you're wrong. I'm going to tell you just how to go about it in your own home using materials you probably have in your garage and kitchen right now. Once you get started, you'll probably decide to add plant propagation to your list of favorite hobbies.

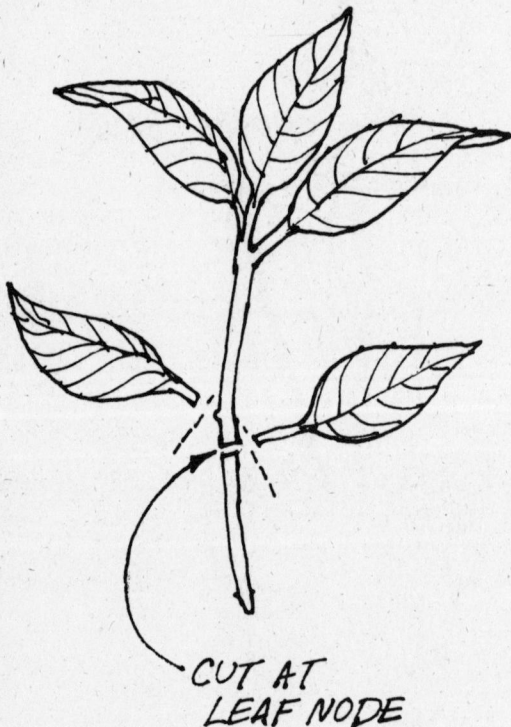

1

SOFT WOOD CUTTING

CUT AT LEAF NODE

You Can't Slip Up with Slips

I told you about Grandma Putt and her slips. Well, slips is just a comfortable, old-fashioned word for cuttings.

Many types of cuttings are used in propagating plants, but I'm just going to talk about those applicable to house plants—namely soft-wood and leaf cuttings. Soft-wood cuttings (also called stem cuttings) are used with soft-stemmed plants like coleus and geraniums and with the new, soft growth of shrubby plants like fuchsia and heliotrope. Leaf cuttings are taken from fleshy-leaved plants, such as African violets and begonias, and from most of the cacti and succulents.

Taking soft-wood cuttings is actually the best method of propagation for a large majority of house plants. It is generally less time-consuming and tedious than starting slow-growing plants from seed, and the results are more reliable.

Everybody has his own ideas on the best time to take soft-wood cuttings, so you'll have to experiment a little—which is always half the fun. Personally, I like to take cuttings either in the early spring sometime around March, or in August. The best way to determine whether time is right for taking cuttings is to test the maturity of the stem. If it is either too old and woody or too young and soft, your efforts will very likely result in failure. It's easy to tell if the stem is ripe—just snap it between your fingers. If it breaks cleanly or only hangs by a bit of tissue, the plant is at the right stage for making cuttings. If the stem bends but doesn't break, it's either too old or too young—you'll know which one by the texture.

Now you're ready to make the cutting. Steel yourself! Remember, you're not amputating; you're pruning and creating new plantlets. Explain to your favorites that you want to preserve their beauty for posterity. They'll understand.

You can use a sharp knife, a small pair of clippers, or a razor blade to take the cuttings. For safety's sake, I use clippers or a knife to cut the shoot off the parent plant; then I make a clean cut with a razor blade.

Don't use stems on which blossom buds have formed. They will root, but they'll embarrass you by growing into anemic-looking, second-rate plants.

Your cuttings should be from two to six inches in length, depending on the size of the plant from which you take them. Remove all the lower leaves from the cutting and, using your razor blade, make a clean, straight cut

2 PUT IN MOIST ROOTING MEDIUM

3 WRAP IN PLASTIC BAG

right at the node (a spot where a leaf was attached to the stem.) This exposes fresh, unbruised cells and encourages the formation of a callus, which is a lot like a scab. If a callus doesn't form, the cutting won't develop roots. Next, dip the cut end of the shoot in Rootone or another of the many commercial rooting powders.

Now you're ready to put your cuttings into a moist rooting medium. I use either perlite or a mixture of equal parts of coarse sand and vermiculite. I sterilize the sand by pouring boiling water over it.

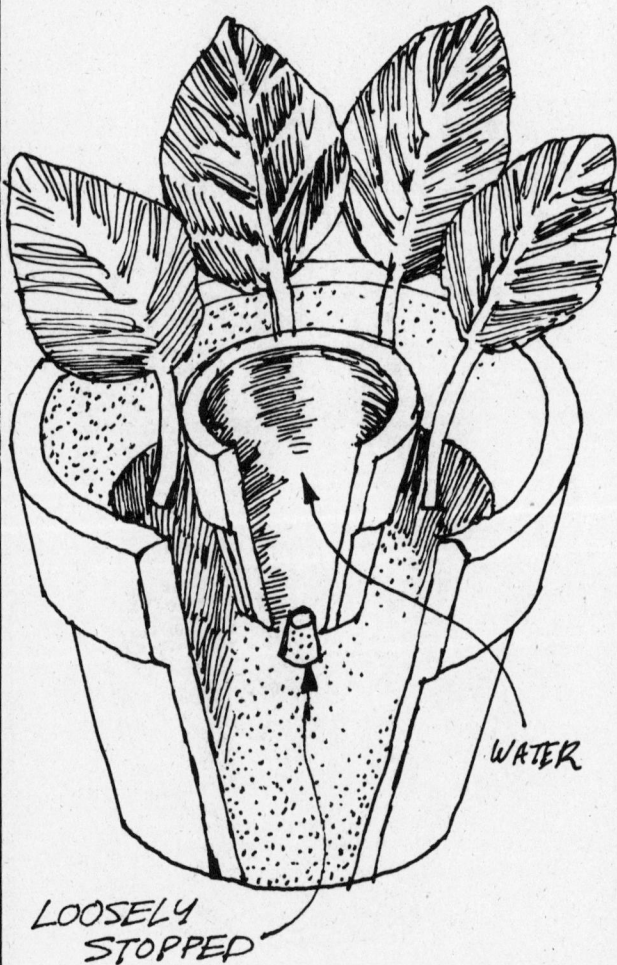

TECHNIQUE FOR KEEPING ROOTING MEDIUM PROPERLY MOIST

WATER

LOOSELY STOPPED

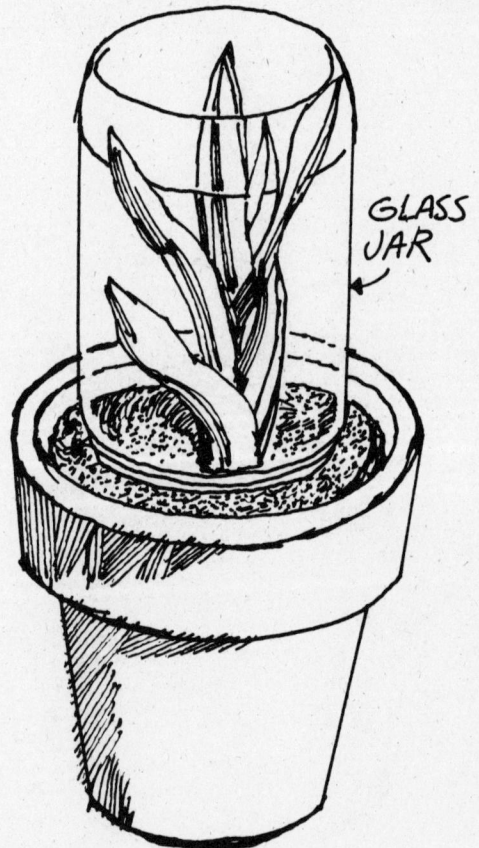

GLASS JAR CAN BE USED OVER CUTTING INSTEAD OF PLASTIC BAG

GLASS JAR

"He goes to pieces every time Mrs. Jones starts making cuttings."

If you want to root a lot of cuttings, try the roll method. Place moist sphagnum on a strip of plastic, insert the cuttings, roll up the plastic and tie with strings.

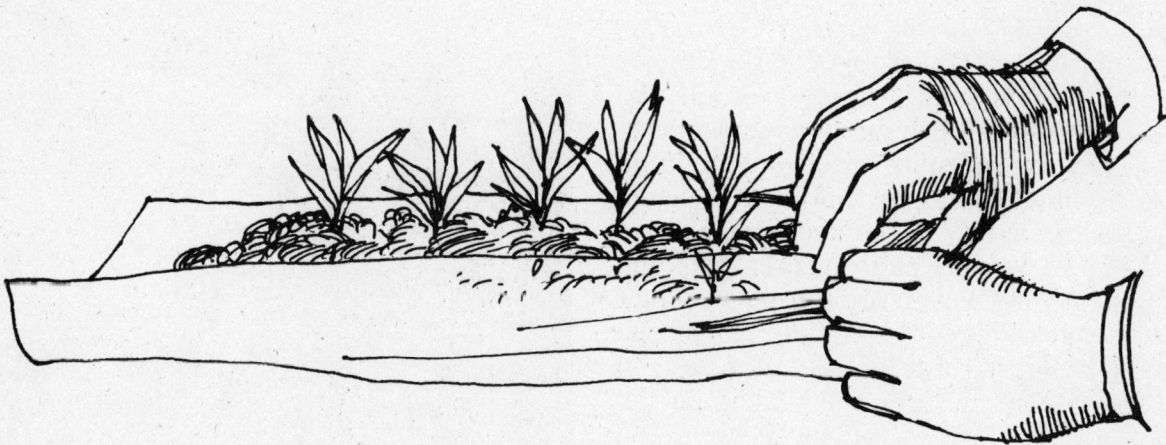

It's easier than you think to root a cutting, and you'll have a lovely free plant.

Choosing a Kindergarten

Many different types of containers are good for rooting cuttings. Purchased or homemade flats, coffee cans, and bulb pans (shallow clay pots) are some of the containers you might use. If you're using tin cans, punch several holes in the bottom and one or two on the sides, just above the bottom edge. When I use bulb pans, I place a small clay pot (with the drainage hole plugged) in the center of the pan. Once the cuttings are planted around the edge, I keep the small pot filled with water, which seeps through and keeps the rooting medium moist. First cover the bottom of your container with drainage material—pebbles or pot shards. Cover this with a mixture of 1 part loam, 2 parts peat moss and 3 parts sand, leaving room at the top of the pot for an inch or two of your perlite or sand-vermiculite rooting medium. Water the filled container thoroughly, insert the cuttings, and firm the medium around them. Take a large plastic freezer bag and turn it upside down over the container. Don't fasten it too tightly—this might cause the humidity to become excessively high. If you do notice a lot of moisture condensing on the inside of the bag, take it off for a while and turn it inside out before replacing it.

Keep the cuttings in a light place but out of direct sunlight. Keep the rooting medium moist but not soaking wet. Bottom heat will speed up rooting. If you don't have electric heating cables, you can easily rig up a heating device by placing a light bulb under an upside-down bulb pan. Set the containers on the bulb pan.

When the cuttings have rooted, you'll have to help them get accustomed to the rigors of everyday living. Leave the bag open for a few hours at first, then keep increasing the time of exposure. When the bag can be left open all day, remove it, and set the plants in a bright window or under lights for about a week. Don't place the young plants in direct sunlight, though.

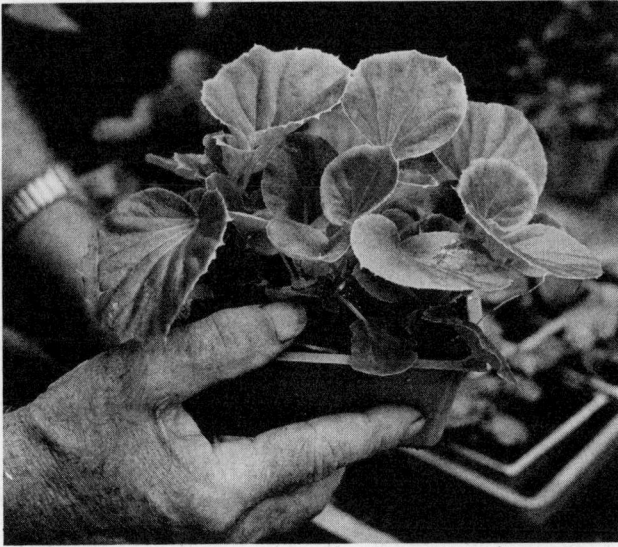

Putting Down Roots

Some plants, including ivy and African violets, will form roots in water. However, it is a much better idea to root these plants in sand or some other solid rooting medium. Water-formed roots have a hard time adjusting themselves to growing in soil once they've become adapted to a more aquatic lifestyle. Even if the plants survive the transition from water to soil, they'll be considerably slowed down by it.

When taking cuttings of succulent plants (like Christmas cacti), it's best to leave them undisturbed for at least 24 hours in a warm, dry place before placing them in a rooting medium. This gives the cut surface time to seal over, which is necessary to rooting.

Individual leaves of semi-succulent plants, like African violets and gloxinias, can be used to form new plants. Cut off a leaf and stalk with a razor blade and dip the end in rooting powder. Insert the cutting (at a slant) into your usual rooting medium. Place the container in a plastic bag and leave it there for about a week. After removing it, water lightly but regularly and mist the leaves occasionally.

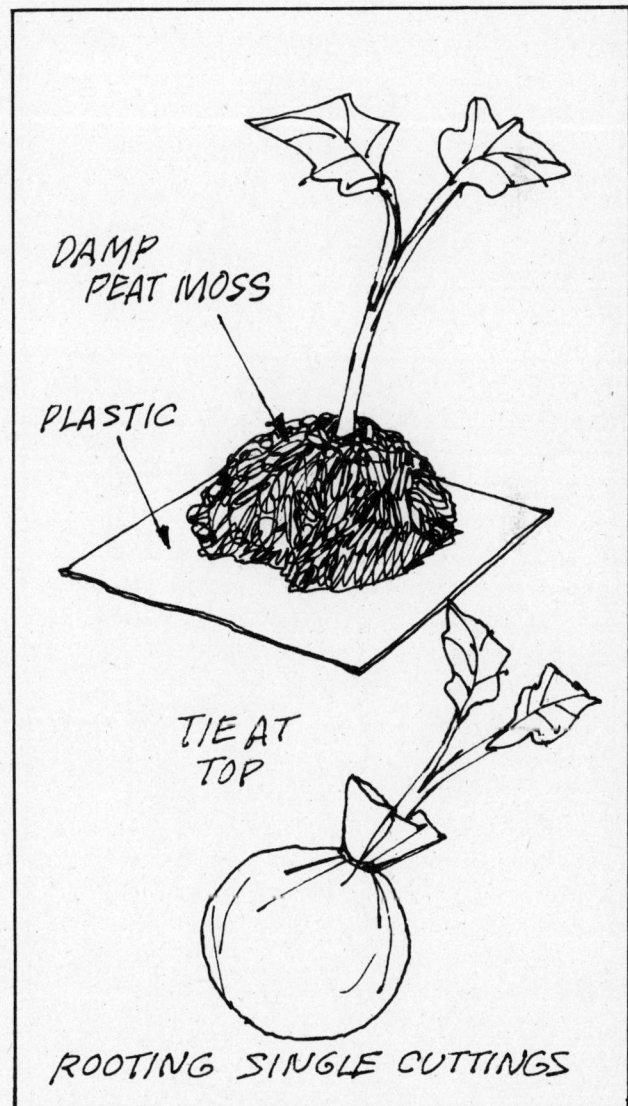

DAMP PEAT MOSS

PLASTIC

TIE AT TOP

ROOTING SINGLE CUTTINGS

Off to a Flying Start

Houseplants which do not receive as much light as they would like are notorious for growing "leggy." Such a plant may prove to be an excellent subject for you to try out your skill at air-layering. Prune the plant back to a reasonable size and at the same time obtain a new plant or two very quickly.

In air-layering, the cutting is not detached from the parent plant until roots have actually formed on it. These plants do not operate on their own until they are able to "root" for themselves. Once cut and planted as an individual they are off to a flying start.

This method of propagation is receiving a lot more attention since plastic bags have come on the market, as these make it a lot easier. The method is quite simple. For our purpose we will use a rubber plant—one of the easiest for an amateur to handle successfully.

Decide where you would like the roots to form, and force the blade of a penknife through the center of the stem. This part of the operation will be easier if you lay the plant on its side. And be sure to explain what you're doing so the plant won't think you're bent on stabbing it to death.

Leave the penknife where it is, then, with a second knife, scrape away the cambium, or outer layer of the stem an inch or two above and below the cut. Do not completely girdle the stem or you'll kill the plant. If there is a milky exudation of sap wipe it away with a paper towel. Now twist the knife blade in the wound, insert a toothpick or kitchen match to hold it open, and remove the knife carefully. Moisten a handful or two of sphagnum moss and wring it lightly so most of the water will be retained. Wrap the moss around the wounded area and tie it firmly into place. Cover it with polyethylene, or wrap a large plastic bag around it. Tie it securely at the bottom, but leave a small opening at the top so water may be added if necessary. Water the mother plant sparingly while the air-layering material is in place to

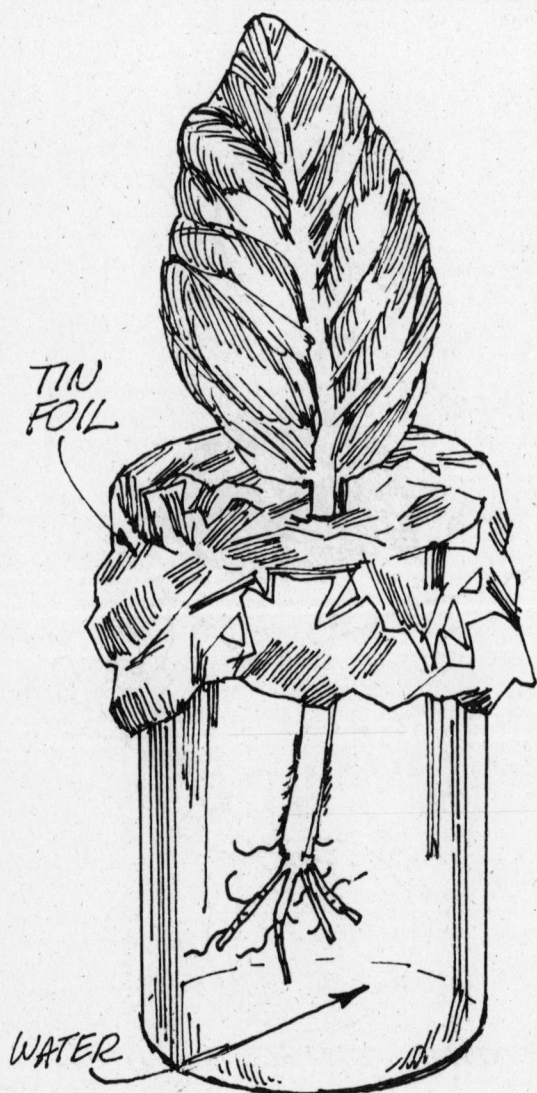

TIN FOIL

WATER

encourage rooting where the plant is obtaining moisture.

It takes six weeks to two months for most plants to fill the moss with roots. When this has taken place, sever the rooted tip from the parent stem and place it in a pot, being careful not to disturb the roots.

Many plants which are difficult to root from cuttings, such as dracaena, diffenbachia, rubber plants and philodendrons, may be quite easily rooted by air-layering. Air-layering is good gardening fun. And it is something that interests children, since the roots can usually be seen through the clear plastic.

To obtain new rex begonia plants you can cut across the larger veins on the underside of the mature leaf. Peg the leaf down to damp sand and new plants will appear at each cut.

AIR-LAYERING

SPHAGNUM WRAPPED IN POLYETHYLENE FILM

CUT OFF AND PLANT

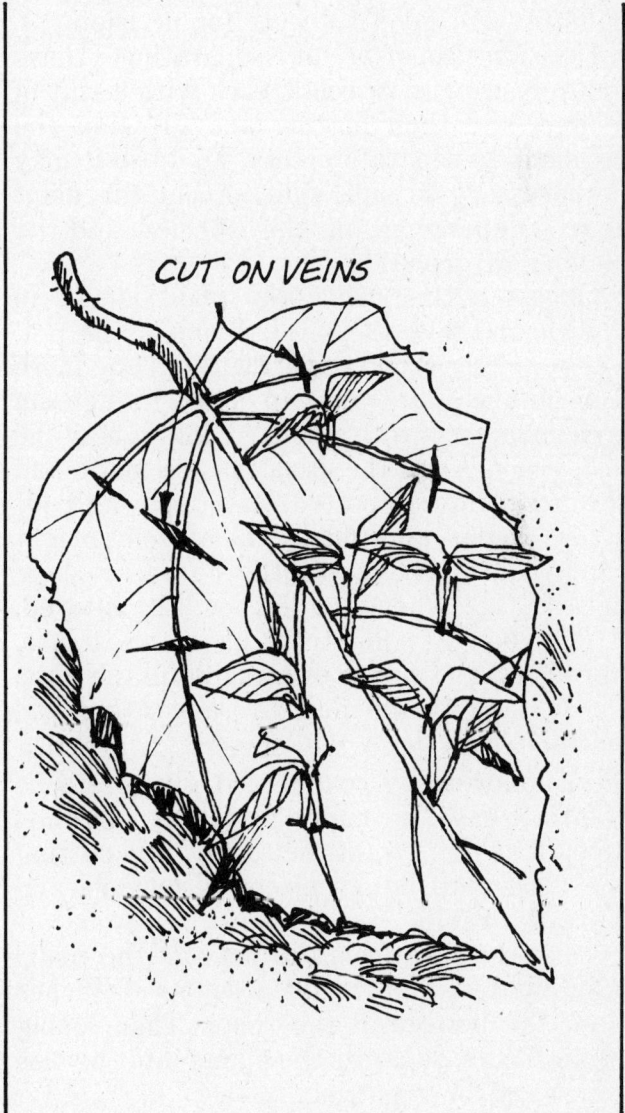

CUT ON VEINS

How Many Crowns Do You Need?

When dividing plants, pry the crowns apart with your fingers or, if they're densely interwoven, use a sharp knife.

Division is the most natural method of propagation for some plants, and this is best accomplished with most species in late winter or early spring when new growth becomes apparent. This is one of the easiest forms of propagation and one most likely to meet with success. Close examination of many of your plants at this time often reveals that they have begun to split themselves into several crowns. African violets, snake-plants and aspidistras are good subjects for division.

Division consists of separating these multiple crowns, or roots, each with a tuft of foliage, and then potting and growing the divisions as separate plants. To do so it may be necessary to pull, split, or cut the plant apart, depending on the species and its manner of growth.

Choose a time when the plant is not in flower, and take the soil ball out of the pot. Try to pry the crowns apart without any more root injury than you can help, though an occasional cut with a sharp knife may be necessary. After the divisions are made and the new plants are potted, water sparingly for a few weeks and shade them from bright sunlight. If you have an outdoor area, set them under a tree where the light will be filtered.

The roots of some ferns grow into dense, fibrous masses which eventually fill the pots. These may be divided by separating the matted roots with the fingers, a practice often followed by commercial growers who want to have as many plants as possible. Most of us don't want that many, and cutting the mass into larger pieces is quicker and more desirable.

Take the fern from the pot (by the usual hard thump), and cut off a couple of inches from the bottom of the roots. Then, using vertical cuts, separate the plants into the size you want for repotting.

Planting Seeds
Is Sow Sow

Plants, like people, are of two sexes and no matter how much the hybridizers continue to fiddle around, it still "takes two to tango." Many plants can be propagated from seed very successfully.

Germination takes place when the seed comes in contact with the moisture and the enzymes within it begin to break down the seed coat. In addition to adequate moisture, air and temperature, among other things, must be in correct balance for the particular plant being grown. Darkness, or subdued light, also plays an important part.

Seeds are relatively inexpensive, so you can have many more different plants than if you buy full-grown plants from a florist or greenhouse. So exercise some patience! Growing plants from seed can be even more exciting than propagation by cuttings or division. And there is a special pride, too, in watching a tiny homegrown plant grow to maturity.

Dampened Spirits

But it isn't fun to come in some morning and see that your little darlings have fallen over during the night, a victim of "that ol' devil," damping off. This condition is caused by various fungus organisms living in the soil and may strike before the seedlings emerge, in which case they either do not reach the surface at all or reach it in such a weakened condition that they do not live. Or it may strike post-emergence. The seedlings do fine for a while and then, quite suddenly, fall over and shrivel up.

There are several ways to defeat this heartless killer of young plants. You can sterilize the soil by baking, by steaming or by the use of boiling water. One of the simplest methods is as follows. Pass the soil mixture through a ¼- to ½-inch sieve. Fill the pots and prepare them for sowing. Water twice with boiling water, and let the soil cool. Then scatter the seeds over the surface, press them in with a tamping tool, and cover them with additional sterilized soil or sand, or vermiculite.

Take a piece of plastic wrap large enough to completely encase the container, top, bottom and sides. Fold the wrap around the container and seal any loose edges. What you have is an "incubation" unit. The moisture contained in the chamber will condense on the plastic wrap and fall back onto the surface, keeping the water supply largely constant.

Place the unit in a dark, warm spot. If placed over a steam or warm air register the seedlings may show up withing 24 to 48 hours. If this is not possible, keep the unit in a room at a temperature around 85 degrees.

When the seedlings become really visible, move the unit to a partially lighted spot— near a window but not in direct sunlight. You may lift one or two edges of the wrap, but otherwise leave it intact.

After a few days, move the seedlings to a cooler location. If the seedlings are kept too warm, they will grow leggy, and this tall spindly growth is extremely brittle, making them more difficult to transplant without breaking. Keep a close watch and remove the plastic film completely when the second set of leaves appears. Once the second set develops, transplant the seedlings into pots or larger flats. Do not put them in pots any larger than necessary.

Pry up the seedlings gently, using a dibble, pencil or spoon, and transplant carefully. Immediately after potting, water the transplants. Keep them in a cool, well-lighted spot. Continue to repot the transplants whenever they need more room, and move them to their permanent locations whenever they're large enough.

Mini-Plants

Up to this point we've been talking about the full-size plants. Now let's look at the possibilities of miniature plants and plants grown in terrariums and fish bowls.

Miniatures are usually grown in shallow containers, sometimes called "dish gardens." These containers without covers have tremendous appeal. With a little imagination you can create a complete garden in miniature. These scenes can be anything you want them to be—oriental, tropical, desert or woodland. These miniature gardens are perfect for people who live in apartments or homes with little room for plants. They also grow beautifully and easily under artificial light.

Designing these gardens is not complicated. Just remember that each small plant must be chosen with great care because each plays an important part in the total design. If you make mistakes, correct them the next time around—a miniature garden is not forever. Its life depends upon the plants, the

"This is very nice, but could I have a room with a little more privacy?"

soil, the temperature, the humidity and your own cultural practices. If you gather plants in a cool section of the country and move them to a warm, dry atmosphere, their life may be short.

Choose a container in keeping with the design you've planned—or plan a garden to fit the container you've bought. The container should be large enough to contain at least three or four plants of contrasting shape, size and color. Make some provision for drainage, either by holes in the bottom or by using some drainage material. If you use drainage material, be sure to water with extreme care to avoid waterlogging. Good drainage materials are broken pot shards, bits of crumbled brick, small pieces of charcoal, gravel, coarse sand or cinders. On top of the drainage material, put a layer of sheet moss to prevent the soil from sifting down and clogging the drainage. Be sure to use the right type of soil even though the dish garden is expected to have only a short life.

Some attractive additions to your garden might be small, lichen-covered rocks. You find interesting shells, bits of decomposing bark, and logs covered with attractive and unusual mosses. On a trip to Colorado, I once found some very odd mosses shaped like little trumpets and I kept them alive in a dish for several months.

Plants Under Glass

You can succeed with a terrarium, for it will grow inside its glass and thrive even with your green thumb tied behind your back. A terrarium is simply a glass-enclosed garden which contains plants or both plants and animals. It keeps life-giving conditions almost perfect by bottling up the climate, providing a moisture-perfect, dust-free space where plants thrive. They have no problems with drafts or gases and are seldom bothered by insects.

A terrarium can be any shape, provided it is a clear container. A fruit jar, a glass dish, a brandy snifter, glass cookwear and even clear plastic may be used. All terrariums, with the exception of cactus gardens, need a glass cover and should be provided with one.

Ferns are especially nice for terrariums and low-growing mosses are ideal, for a terrarium is a spot where wall-to-wall planting may be practiced with good results. Mosses, cut and shaped, may also make a lining for your container, or you may drape them over small rocks. Liverworts, small green plants similar to mosses, also do well. These grow on damp ground, in water or on tree trunks.

Tiny shrubs and trees that are just starting to sprout from seeds are good choices, especially if your terrarium is to be the woodland type. Look for cedar, white pine and hemlock. Seedlings of deciduous trees, such as birch, maple and oak, may also be used. Simply replace them when they outgrow their allotted space. Low-growing plants and vines, creeping fig and partridge berry are also candidates.

The first step in any hobby is to organize your materials. Arrange the plants you have decided to use in several ways before you place them in your planter. Doing this before you place them inside will keep from smearing the glass by too much moving around. And keeping the glass or plastic clean is the first rule of terrarium planting. These surfaces are difficult to clean after the plants are in place.

Use about a half inch of charcoal in the bottom of the terrarium. Since this is a nondrainage planter, the charcoal helps keep the soil sweet. Place moist soil in the container. Do not smear the glass. Tilt the container so the mix is higher on one side than the other. This provides a natural "hillside" instead of a flat background.

Plant the taller plants first. Dig the hole off center on the uphill side to give more root depth. Spread the roots evenly and cover with soil. Tamp with a wood dowel or a cork attached to a stiff wire. Spray the plants lightly with water. Let the earth soak up the water, then test to see if a bit of moisture comes out when the material is pressed down with your finger. If it does, you've watered enough.

Continue planting toward the foreground, putting small ground covers in last. Remember to leave open spaces—let nature have some fun. Don't fill it all up.

For most terrariums the ideal temperature is 70 to 75 degrees, daytime; 59 to 60 degrees at night. You may give them an hour or two of sunlight in the early morning or the late afternoon. For the greater part of the day, though, a woodland terrarium should be placed in a shaded spot.

Within twenty-four hours after you finish planting, the closed terrarium will have a slight mistiness around the top. This is normal. High humidity and coolness at night, plus warmth by day, will suit your plants just fine.

Desert-planted terrariums do best in a daytime temperature of 75 to 85 degrees and a nighttime temperature not lower than 65. These plants need long hours of sunlight, especially during the winter months. Remember, however, that the action of the sun will dry out the terrarium more quickly, so keep watch. Never let the soil mix dry out completely.

The only thing more fun than growing a plant is sharing one.

Plants Are for Giving

Just about everybody who starts thinking "Christmas gift plant" immediately envisions poinsettias. You may not know, though, that while red is still the most popular color, you now have a choice of varying shades—white, pink, or even marbeled!

Poinsettias can be enjoyed longer if a few simple suggestions for their care are followed. Check the soil every day and water when it feels dry. Don't allow it to dry out completely—or remain soaked. Make sure the drainage hole is not plugged. Place your plant near a warm, sunny window, but don't let it touch the glass. Keep your plant away from extreme heat or cold and out of drafts. Feed it a soluble fertilizer after a month or so.

When you get tired of your poinsettia, after the leaves fall off, stop watering and store it in a cool, dry place. In spring, water it again and cut the stems back to six inches. Keep the stems pinched back as new leaves begin to form. From early October until blooming starts, place the plant in a dark closet for 12 hours each day and keep in a

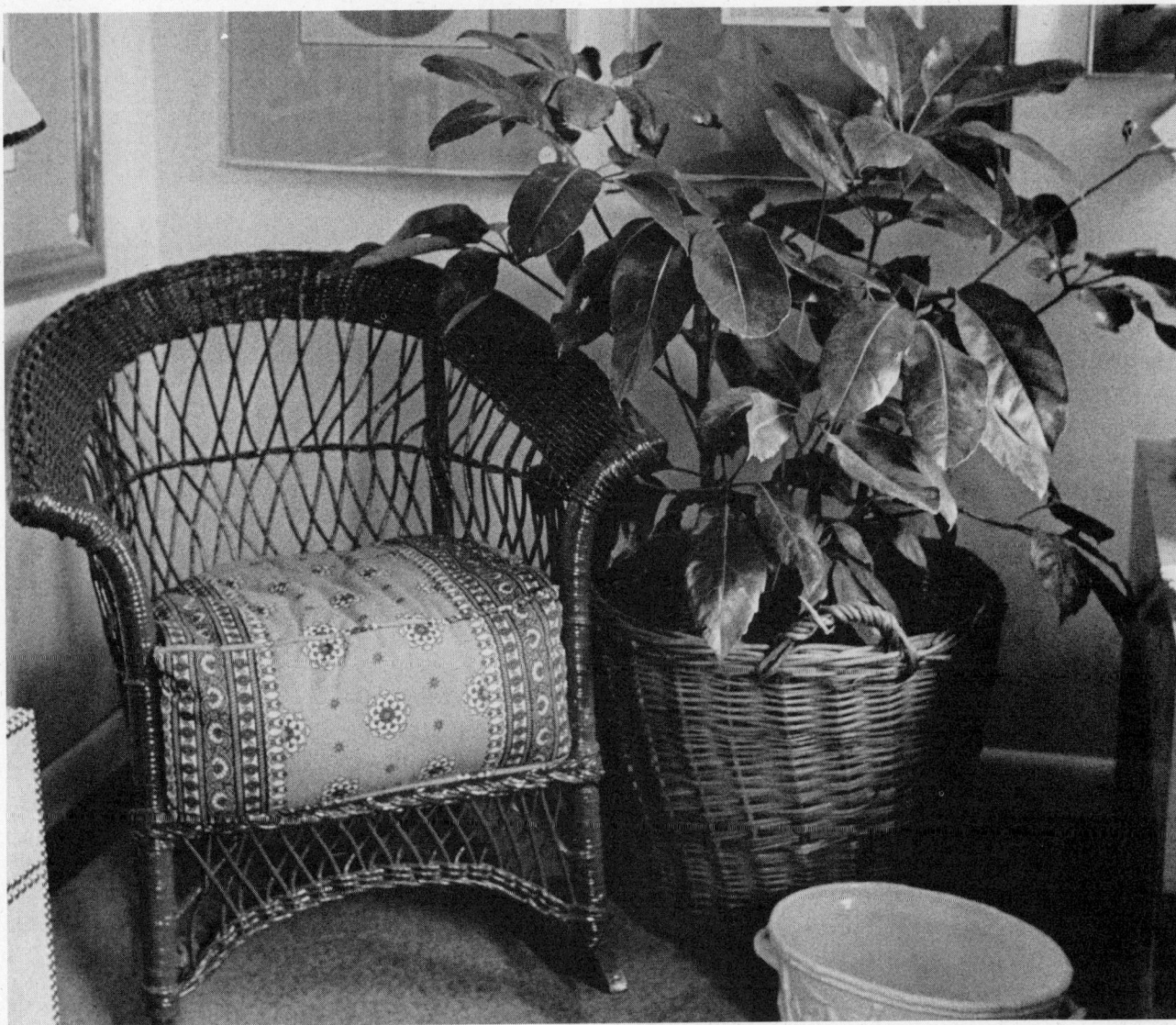

sunny window for the other 12 hours of the day. Fertilize during the active growth.

Chrysanthemums are another favorite gift plant, for they are usually the longest-lasting flowering plants. Keep yours in good light and in the coolest spot you have. Night temperatures of 60 to 65 degrees are especially important to chrysanthemums. One way to give the plant a cooler atmosphere is to set it on the floor when you go to bed. Be sure, though, that it's not in a draft.

Water it well and frequently—about every other day, or when the soil becomes dry. If the plant is in a soilless medium, as some are now grown, give it a soluble fertilizer feeding

after you have had it for about a month. Be sure it gets enough sunshine. Spray it with water frequently—keeping its leaves clean will make it prettier and more comfortable. After your plant has stopped blooming cut it back to about 8 inches and keep it moist, but not wet. Hardy varieties can be planted outside, but many are tender and must be planted in well-protected spots and covered closely if you want to carry them over winter.

Agile Azaleas

Azaleas are seen more and more frequently as gift plants and they are being offered in both single and semi-double varieties. Azaleas need bright light but not strong sun. The soil should be evenly moist and the temperature kept between 55 and 65 degrees. This may mean putting them on the floor or in a cooler room. You'll have better luck in keeping your azalea if you remove the foil or other covering from the pot and submerge the pot in a pan of water every other day for fifteen to twenty minutes, then allow it to drain. Spray the foliage with water three or four times a week.

To get azaleas to bloom another year is a bit tricky. They need a six weeks' cool treatment—around 40 degrees. Give the plant a chance to replenish its strength after it has finished blooming. In the summer, set the pot in the ground in semi-shade where it is protected from hot, drying winds. Water it regularly and feed it with special fertilizer for acid-loving plants. Bring it inside in early fall and place it in a cool, light place, keeping the soil moist but not wet. When buds show activity, provide more sun, water and fertilizer.

Easter lilies like it cool, so keep them well out of the sun and check daily to see if the soil is drying out. When it seems sandy on top, water well. Make sure the pot drains well.

To keep lilies looking well, remove blossoms as they fade and pinch out the yellow anthers as new buds open. After the last blossom falls you should still keep your plant watered and in good light. Eventually it will die down.

If you want it to bloom again indoors, plant the bulb in a pot with only two inches of soil beneath the bulb. Place it in an unheated garage until December, then bring it indoors and keep at a temperature no higher than 60 degrees.

Hydrangeas bloom for a long time if you keep them well watered and out of direct sun. Water at least twice a day or submerge the pot in a pan of water daily, and then drain. After your plant has finished blooming, cut back all the stems which bore flowers, then plant it in your garden in a shady spot. The stems that have not bloomed will often produce blooms during the summer.

If you bring the plant back inside for winter, cut it back severely after it has bloomed, and repot in fresh planter mix. Keep it in full sun, give it a great deal of water and feed it with fish tablets once a week.

Keep Cyclamens Cool

If someone presents you with a cyclamen, you really have a plant worthy of cherishing and it is not really difficult to keep. Keep it in a cool (50 to 60 degrees), bright place where the humidity is high. Pay particular attention to giving it a cool atmosphere at night; a temperature of 55 degrees at night enables it to stand warmer temperatures in the day.

When your plant needs watering, stand the pot in a basin of water until the top of the soil shows dampness. Allow to drain. With good care these beauties may continue to bloom from Christmas up to May.

When your cyclamen ceases flowering, the leaves will begin to turn yellow. This does not mean the plant is dying but is a signal that it

To prolong blooming, keep lilies cool and water them well.

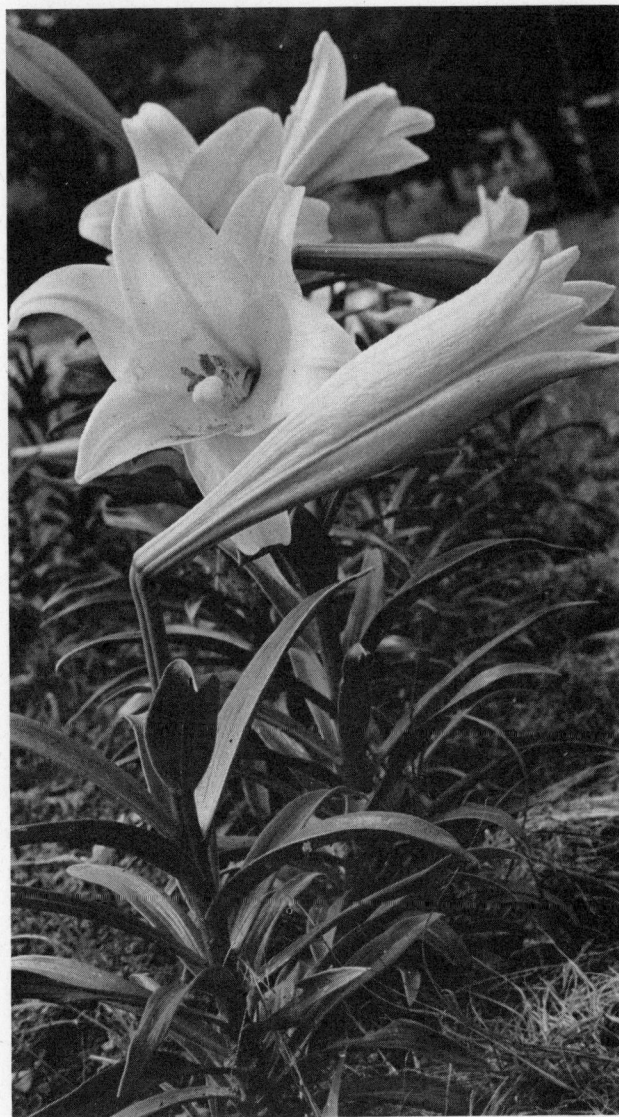

anything—people, animals or plants—you become sensitive to each other. They grow accustomed to your way of caring for them and come to depend upon it. As you care for your plants, you learn their language and begin to interpret their needs.

As time goes on, confidence and respect develop between you. I think this becomes especially true of gift plants, for they are nearly always a gift from a loved one to a loved one. With the atmosphere so cordial to begin with, it's likely to remain so. And I think that plants, like children, feel this and grow best in a happy home.

wants to rest. Clean away all the dead growth from the corms and reduce the water supply. Around the last of May, cease watering entirely and expose the pot to full light until about the first of August, then begin watering. When you notice young leaves developing, repot in the next size container and return the plant to the window sill.

Gloxinias are handsome house plants with velvety flowers in many deep, dramatic colors. With proper care, they will last for months. They require full light but should never be placed directly in the sun. Keep the soil uniformly moist. This is best done by setting the pot in a pan of water and letting it seep upward. If you must water from the top, do not wet the foliage.

The gloxinia you get from the florist will quite likely be a two-year-old plant, raised from seed or cutting. These plants are tropical so you should never put them where the temperature will drop below 50 degrees.

Plants do have personalities and there is no doubt that we grow fonder of some than others. Do they know this? I think they do and often respond to us the same way. I believe they have feelings and will often do better for someone they like. And they may even pout and become stubborn if they build up a dislike.

When you are in close contact with

Pruning

Your living room landscape should be in balance and resemble a lovely indoor garden—don't let it become a jungle!

By now your plants have become established, they have warmed up to you and you to them. Quite likely they want to please you and will reward all your good care by a tremendous surge of growth. Sometimes this seems to take place almost overnight, but it was really going on all the time. Maybe you just didn't notice because you were so pleased with all the new leaves, branches, buds and flowers that were forming—as indeed you have a right to be. But sometimes, enough is enough.

Don't let the words "pruning" or "training" frighten you. Just think what you would look like if you didn't cut your fingernails occasionally! Plants are the same way, they need to be manicured.

Pinching a plant is simply removing the tip of a growing shoot. This is usually done by

Pinching out the growing tips keeps a plant compact and bushy. To control a plant's shape, prune back branches to buds facing in the direction you want growth to take.

pressing it off with the thumbnail and finger. The reason for pinching is to restrain the over-enthusiastic plant and to promote a compact, bushy habit of growth. Pinching checks the strong shoots and stimulates into growth the buds which might otherwise have remained dormant. Disbudding, another form of pinching, is the removal of flower buds so the plant is forced to conserve its energy until you want it to bloom.

Pruning is more severe than pinching and involves more cutting back. It may also include root pruning as well as pruning the upper growth. Whichever is in order for a particular plant, do it with a sharp knife or

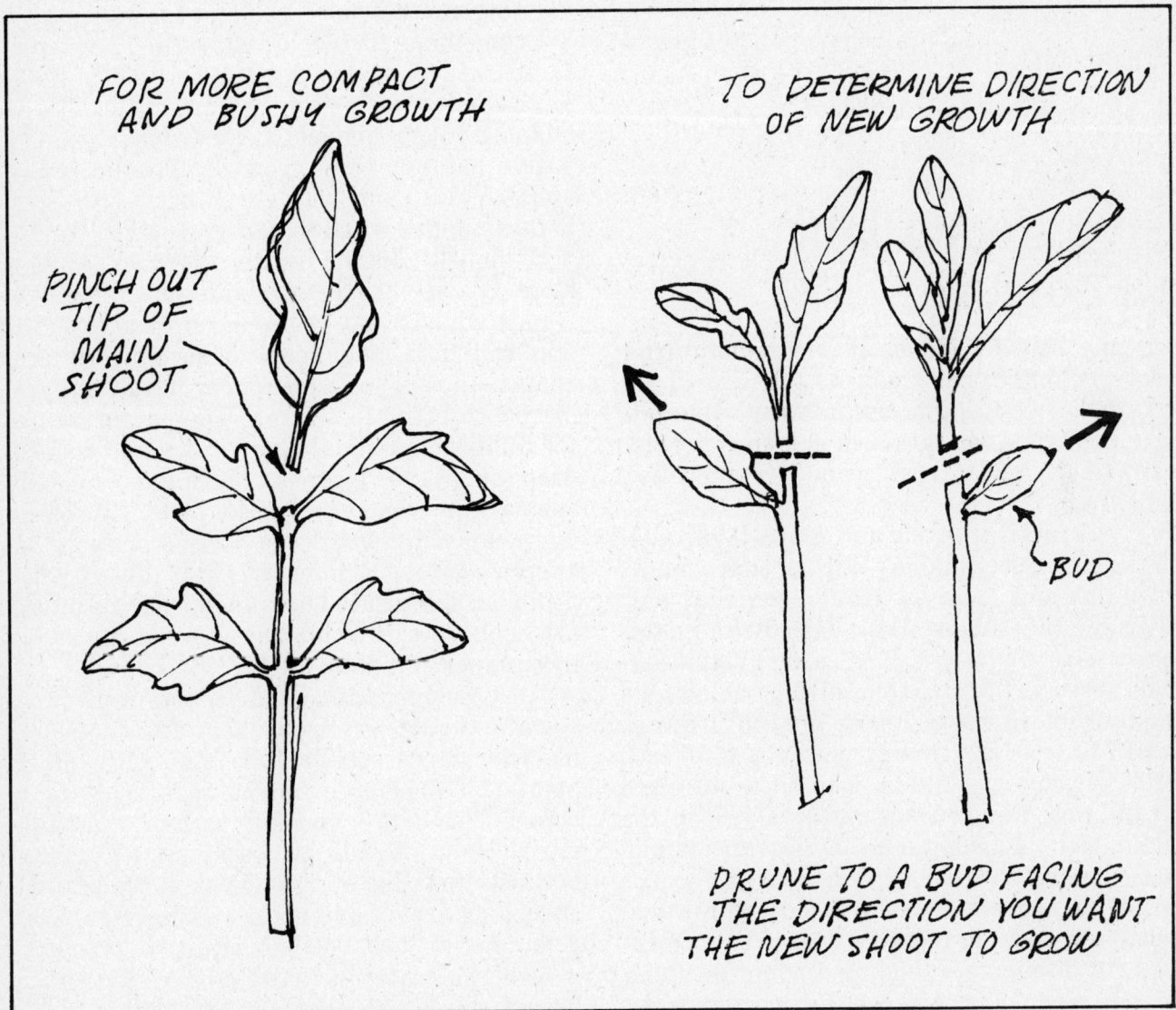

FOR MORE COMPACT AND BUSHY GROWTH

TO DETERMINE DIRECTION OF NEW GROWTH

PINCH OUT TIP OF MAIN SHOOT

BUD

PRUNE TO A BUD FACING THE DIRECTION YOU WANT THE NEW SHOOT TO GROW pruning shears. Never hack at a plant with dull tools.

When pruning back a branch, make your cuts just above a bud pointed in the direction that you want the bush to develop. If a branch needs to be completely removed, cut it close to the trunk or parent branch; do not leave a stub.

If you need to prune back a diseased portion, cut back to healthy tissue. Be sure to disinfect your tools with denatured alcohol before using them again.

Give Your Plant a Pedicure

Many healthy indoor plants benefit from root pruning, which reduces the size of the root ball so it can go back into the same pot. The best time for this is in the spring when growth is most active and wounds heal quickly.

Knock out the plant and place it on your potting bench or table. With a sharp knife, trim portions from all around the root ball. (Water the plant the day before this operation so you will have a fairly compact ball to work with.) Avoid letting the soil fall away from the roots. Shape the root mass so it will fit reasonably well, with about an inch or so of room all around, when it is returned to the pot. Repot, using new soil. Keep the plant for a while in a warm, humid atmosphere to give it a chance to recover from its operation. Keep it out of the sun until new roots have had a chance to form. If you cut off a corresponding amount of upper foliage, your plant will recover more quickly.

Bernard Bromeliad

A Bromeliad is any plant belonging to the pineapple family. They make ideal house plants but for some reason are not very well known. If you have ever cut off the top of a fresh pineapple and inserted it in a pot where it obligingly grew, you have grown a Bromeliad. But this plant, however interesting it may have been, is not nearly as exciting as the more colorful forms.

Bromeliads thrive on warmth, and room temperatures never get too hot. They have developed water-retaining powers peculiarly adapted to dry household conditions. In their native habitat, they grow on tree branches and are accustomed to very little light. This makes them ideal for darker rooms.

Billbergia nutans is an evergreen plant from Brazil with long, rigid, pineapple-like leaves which rise, in the form of a rosette, straight from the roots. The flowers are spikes, or panicles, and appear in the centers of the rosettes in winter. The temperature for Billbergias should never be allowed to drop below 55 degrees. Potting is done in spring in a compost of peat, loam, sand and leafmold with a generous portion of chopped charcoal. Pots should be half filled with drainage material. They need a fairly moist atmosphere with abundant water at the roots in summer but less during the winter.

Most Bromeliads are air plants, but they seem to thrive very well when their roots are placed in a coarse planter mix. Also, most plants have pointed leaves that arise in a whorl. This center forms a natural vase and must be kept full of water at all times because the base of the leaves is the water-absorbing area. Save rainwater, refrigerator drippings or use bottled water if you live where the water is hard or heavily chlorinated.

Neoregelia Carolinae

Hieroglyphic Vriesia

Dyckia Fosteriana

Droophead Guzmania

Flowering House Plants

CAMELLIAS

Camellias are much the same as azaleas in their cultural requirements. They need cool temperatures and high humidity. Grow them in a greenhouse, if you have one, and bring them in during the day to be enjoyed, but let them have a cool place to sleep at night. The blooms are so breathtakingly beautiful that they are worth a bit of extra trouble.

Like azaleas, they need an acid soil mix rich in organic matter, such as leaf mold and peat moss. Add a generous amount of charcoal and use cottonseed meal as a fertilizer. The soil should always be kept moist.

Use a mister on hot days to spray the plants to prevent bud drop. Light should be filtered but they should not be kept in deep shade.

GERANIUMS

We have become so accustomed to geraniums that we do not think of them as exotics. And indeed most geraniums dislike being coddled.

Unlike so many plants that originate in the tropics they need an average potting soil, one not overly rich—one part each of sand and humus (peat moss or leaf mold) and two parts of garden loam, with a small amount of fine ground bone meal or super-phosphate, is a perfect mix.

Fertilizers high in nitrogen produce more foliage and fewer flowers. Only when they're getting ready to flower do they need fertilizer—the rest of the time keep the soil packed firmly around their roots. While flowering, add some Ra-Pid-Gro to the water and water a little more often, but try not to splash the water on the flower buds, as they rot easily.

While geraniums like having their leaves sprayed off occasionally, be very stingy with water on the soil. Do not spray the leaves when the sun is on them.

Geraniums love sunshine and enjoy all you can give them, especially in winter. While they do not flower all year long, this obliging plant permits you to choose the season. If you want winter flowers, pinch off any summer flower buds. If you want summer flowers, do not let any flower buds form until after March.

One thing is absolutely necessary if you plan to force your geraniums into bloom, and that is to have them pot-bound. (This means that the pot your plant is in will be allowed to fill itself with roots.) Of course, this condition cannot go on indefinitely, for the roots will force all the soil out of the pot, and the plant will die.

Place several pieces of broken shards in the bottom of the pot to make sure that the drainage hole remains open. Be sure the soil is sifted down around the sides of the pot, leaving no air holes, then water thoroughly.

To avoid ungainly, leggy plants control the growth by pinching back the tips, which encourages branching. Long, weak shoots are the result of too much water, too much fertilizer or too little light.

The most common types of geraniums are the zonal and ivy-leaved varieties which produce white, pink, rose-red and even lavender-colored flowers. Many species of this delightful plant have scented leaves—lemon, nutmeg, rose and peppermint.

Martha Washington geraniums are different in appearance and culture from the others. They resemble azaleas and produce their flowers in large clusters only in the spring, then go into a rest period.

Geranium   Poinsettia

Rex Begonia   Wax Begonia

GARDENIAS

Have you got a "thing" about the romance and mystery of old southern gardens? If so, gardenias are for you!

Gardenia jasminoides (Veitchei), the type most florists offer for use as a pot plant, requires a minimum winter temperature of 60 degrees. Potting compost should consist of peat, loam and well-decomposed manure in equal parts laced with sand and a small quantity of crushed charcoal.

Old plants should be repotted and pruned in February. Set the plants in larger pots, add fresh soil, and sprinkle (or mist) the plants freely. After they become well-established, expose the plants to full sunlight but keep in a moist atmosphere.

The planter mix for gardenias should always be loose and porous. Gardenias are acid-loving plants. When this mix becomes alkaline, from the accumulation of hard-water salts, iron is not available to the roots. The top leaves turn yellow. When this happens, the plant must be provided iron sulfate.

Remove the flower buds during the summer and the plants will bloom in autumn and winter. Water freely in summer and add liquid fertilizer once a week to established plants. Less water is needed in winter, but never let the atmosphere or soil remain dry too long.

FUCHSIAS

Since fuchsias bloom from April to October, they are not only grown as house plants but also in window boxes. The best time to start them for house plants is November or December.

As soon as you get your plants they should be placed in 4- or 5-inch pots. Place bits of broken pot shards over the drainage holes in the bottom to prevent clogging and use a rich, porous soil mixture—1 part garden loam, 1 part sand, 2 parts compost or leafmold, ½ part dried cow manure and 1 tablespoon of bonemeal per quart. Firm the soil about the plant's roots. Water from the bottom by putting the pot in a pan of water and allowing it to soak all the water the soil will hold. Drain for a few minutes and place in a light, but not sunny, window. Leave it in this location until the roots are well-established, then give it a little sun part of the day.

Fuchias should not become pot-bound. Repot frequently, using the next larger size pot each time. They require plenty of light, but should be kept out of the midday sun.

Water freely during their growing season, but decrease the amount gradually from late October to the middle of November. Then repot, cutting back the plants half way, and store in a cool, dark cellar. Give them just enough water to keep the soil from becoming bone-dry until March when the plants should be returned to light and watered generously.

From March on, give a weekly watering with liquid manure or plant food until the first flower bud appears. Pinch back the growing tip often to keep them compact and bushy.

STARFISH PLANT

Stapelia or starfish plant is a branching succulent resembling a cactus but without thorns. The strange star-shaped flowers, nearly two inches across, are spotted yellow and brown.

FUCHSIA

This plant needs plenty of sunlight and water, excellent drainage and a fairly rich, loose soil.

The best potting mixture is 2 parts sand, 2 parts garden loam, 4 parts humus, 1 part of broken flowerpots and 1 tablespoon of bone-meal or limestone per quart of the potting mixture.

During the fall months let the plants rest with less light and water. In early winter, place them in a sunny window and give plenty of water, being sure that the soil does not become soggy. Water frequently but do not leave the pot in a container of water—soil must always be drained. Allow the plants to become root-bound in order to force blooming. Early in March the plants should start to bloom and the blooming season should continue well into summer.

SPATHIPHYLLUM

Spathiphyllums produce both graceful white flowers and very ornamental dark green leaves. They need a moist, tropical atmosphere, for their natural environment is near the equator on the dark jungle floor. The minimum winter temperature should be 55 degrees. They have adjusted to a climate where the seasons are so much the same that there is little need for a rest period or dormancy. For this reason, spathiphyllum blooms almost constantly and thrives in a warm, dark, household interior, making it an ideal house plant.

Most of these plants have erect, lance-shaped leaves varying in length from 6 to 20 inches. The flower spathes, which are produced on short stems, average three inches and are white or greenish-white in color.

Fertilizing regularly with a diluted liquid fertilizer benefits this plant. Repotting, if necessary, should be done in February. Remove the root ball and take off some of the old soil with a pointed stick. Repot in the next largest pot size, adding some new soil.

VENUS FLY TRAP

The Venus fly trap catches and digests its prey in the traps it produces in place of normal leaves. The leafy structure consists of two blades, hinged in the center with interlocking teeth along the margins. Trigger hairs, located on the surface of each blade, operate the mechanism. When the trigger hairs are disturbed, the jaws snap shut to form a tight pouch. Continued irritation by the struggling, entrapped insect causes the leaf glands to exude the digestive fluids that disintegrate the soft tissues of the insect's body.

After several days, or even weeks, with a large insect, when the nutrients have been absorbed into the plant's tissues, the trap reopens and only the skeleton remains. If the trap is purposely or accidentally stimulated it snaps shut, but when it finds itself without a meal it automatically reopens in a few days.

Plant your Venus fly trap in a shallow dish without any drainage, and set the roots in fairly loose, live sphagnum moss. Water frequently and pour off surplus water. High humidity is essential. In homes with dry heat, sufficient humidity can be created by the use of a miniature greenhouse or a terrarium bowl.

The roots must be kept moist at all times and under no circumstances should plant foods or insect sprays be used on this plant.

It grows best in full sunshine but tolerates some shade. When kept in the sun, the leaf traps take on a reddish color.

Stems bearing small, white flowers appear in May or June and should be removed as they are unattractive and tend to weaken the plant. If exposed to extreme cold or allowed to become too dry, the top may die, but under proper growing conditions a new growth cycle will start from the perennial bulb-like root after a few weeks' rest.

VENUS FLY TRAP

FLOWERING MAPLE

Abutilon or flowering maple is a tender shrub having large, deep-green leaves with a striking white margin. It is normally grown indoors as a house plant but also makes an excellent border or window-box specimen. The pendant bell-shaped flowers are rosy-orange, and form during the summer and fall.

The potting soil should be made rich with two-thirds loam and one-third leaf mold and decayed manure. New growth begins in the spring, and plants may be transferred to a slightly larger pot if rootbound. After repotting, it is important to keep them in a warm, damp atmosphere for several weeks, and sprinkle the leaves often.

In their permanent location the plants require full sun and free air circulation. Dropping of the lower leaves indicates a need for fertilization, so make bi-weekly applications of fertilizer during the summer. The soil should be kept in a drier condition in the winter, but the stems should never be allowed to shrivel from a lack of moisture.

Plants grown in pots are pruned in March by shortening last year's growth. They should then be kept in a moist atmosphere with the temperature between 55 and 60 degrees.

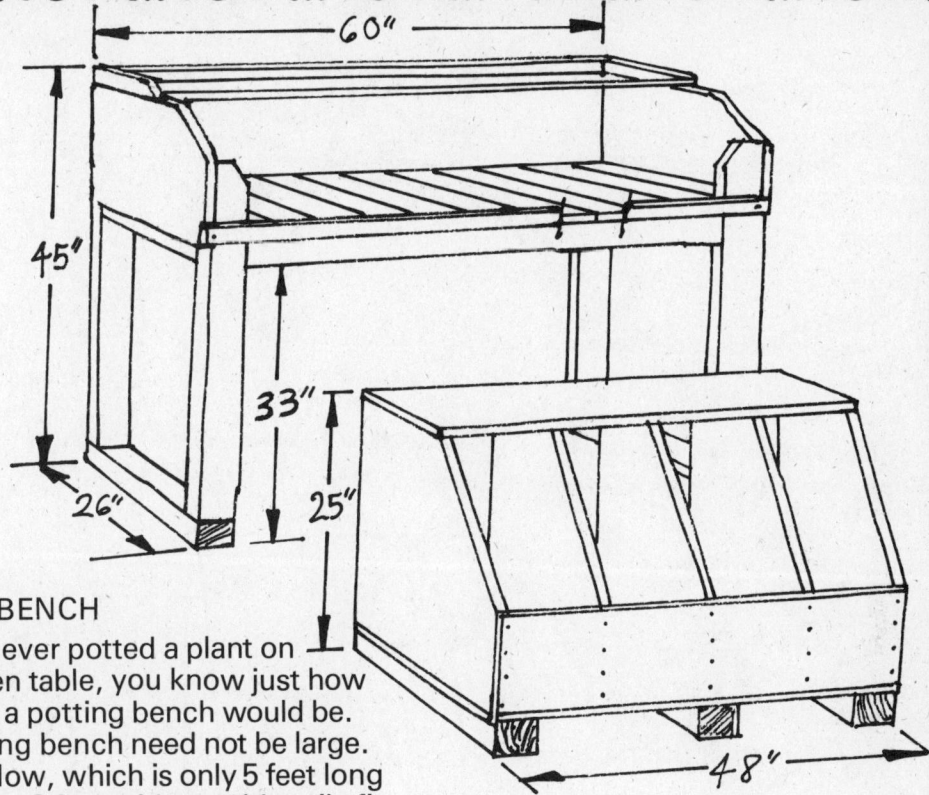

POTTING BENCH

If you've ever potted a plant on your kitchen table, you know just how convenient a potting bench would be. And a potting bench need not be large. The one below, which is only 5 feet long and less than 3 feet wide, could easily fit into a garage or basement. Another advantage of this bench is that the storage bins are not attached to the bench itself. Both are easily portable so the entire work center can be rearranged or moved outdoors whenever you like. Outdoors, the bins, which hold manure, compost, and other potting mixtures, could be protected from rain by a sheet of plastic or canvas mounted on a dowel and tacked to the front edge of the bench.

If you have room, you might build a second simpler bench or some sturdy shelves for storing pots, flats, watering cans and similar equipment. It's a good idea to locate your potting bench near a source of water to make clean-ups and watering easier. It's also a good idea to attach a towel rack or paper towel dispenser on one side of the bench.

Jadeplant

Christmas Cactus

Echeveria

Cotyledon

GREENE

Charlie Cactus

A cactus has just about as many admirers as other plants. And if you believe a cactus is all thorns and prickles, you are in for a big surprise, for a cactus in bloom is not surpassed even by an orchid. Even the lowly prickly pear is crowned with gorgeous, delicate yellow flowers during its annual blooming season—some species even produce orange or red flowers.

The night-blooming cerei (Saguaro, Queen of the Night, Organ Pipe) all have white flowers that open late in the evening and close the following morning. The blossoms of cereus hexagonius are white, tinged with purple on their outer petals, and resemble a magnificent water lily when they are in full bloom.

For indoor cultivation, cacti require a minimum greenhouse temperature of 40 degrees, and 10 or 15 degrees more is even better. With few exceptions, they should be exposed to every bit of available sunlight (or grown under fluorescents) throughout the year.

Cacti are easy to grow, but for those in "captivity" the trick is to persuade them to bloom. Good drainage is essential. Fill the pot a fourth full of flowerpot chips or pea-size gravel before putting in any soil. Succulents and cacti do not, as many think, grow in pure sand. They need a nutritional soil suited to their particular needs. A mix composed of equal parts of garden loam, leaf mold and sand is satisfactory for most species.

For desert-type cacti, add more sand and some gravel; for jungle species, use shredded fir bark or osmunda fiber mixed with one part garden loam. All ingredients should be thoroughly mixed and the texture should be loose and friable so it will drain easily yet provide moisture for the plant roots.

Use pots which seem too small for the plants. There is a good reason for this. Cacti make comparatively few roots and will not bloom in larger pots.

Wear good heavy gloves when you are working with cacti, or fold a newspaper and encircle the plant with the paper. Those spines are what nature gave it for protection.

CHRISTMAS CACTI

The Christmas cactus blooms between November and March. They are easy to grow and sure bloomers if you follow directions. Plant in a pot no larger than 5 inches. Use a gritty, porous soil composed of garden loam, leaf mold and sand, plus a generous sprinkling of well-rotted or dried cow manure. Avoid using any bonemeal or lime.

Put the plants in a permanent place away from direct sun and drafts. Place them in an east or west window. If they must be in a south window, the sun should be diffused through a curtain. Keep the soil almost dry until the flower buds begin to appear. Then water moderately until the plants are through flowering. Reduce the watering as soon as flowering stops in order to give the plants a rest until new shoots start growing. During the resting period, cut off any straggly growth.

Water freely while new growth is forming in the spring. When Christmas cacti drop their flower buds before they open, it is usually because of too much or too little watering, drafts or sudden changes in temperature, manufactured gas in the air or too much handling. Do not move the plants about while the flower buds are developing.

SUCCULENTS

Defining a succulent is a little more difficult than defining a cactus for, while a cactus is a succulent that can store moisture—not all succulents are cacti.

Cacti, with rare exceptions, do not have leaves. But succulents, far from belonging to any one family, may be lilies, amaryllises, daisies, milkweeds, crassulas and even geraniums. But there are interesting and often very dramatic types among these, and no book on house plants would be complete without describing some of them.

Pot culture for most succulents is similar to that of cactus; many of them are propagated in much the same manner by removing suckers from the base of the plants and potting them as individuals.

Aloe Vera, a diversified succulent, which is a sort of drugstore in a flowerpot, is not new. In the tropics it has been known, used and respected for centuries. It is now being made into all kinds of creams and lotions here in the United States. It is a great remedy for painful but not too severe burns, minor skin irritations, innocuous insect bites, minor sunburn and chapped hands.

Aloe Vera is an interesting-looking plant that practically takes care of itself. It has fierce-looking, lance-shaped leaves with jagged edges set with spines. The spines are not nearly so sharp as they look and the soft barbs do not "hook."

For pot culture, fill the container with about a fourth drainage material, the rest of the mixture should be about two-thirds loam and one-third coarse sand. Add a little crushed limestone and bonemeal.

Pot in the spring and water sparingly in the summer, only when the soil becomes quite dry. From September to March give only enough water to prevent the leaves from shriveling.

Opal Orchid

Many people hesitate to attempt orchids, believing them too delicate. As with other species of plants there are some that are easier to grow than others. Much depends upon where you live, how you live and what facilities you can provide for their growth.

In southern California tender orchids, such as Cymbidiums, are grown in garden beds of specially prepared soil. In Florida many epiphytal kinds are grown on trees out of doors. Provision must be made to protect them from extremely low temperatures. On nights when such conditions may be expected, hoods of heavy cloth are put over the plants. Even in the warm parts of the United States orchid growing is most successful if practiced indoors. Orchids are more exacting in their requirements than most house plants, so conditions favorable to their culture must be provided and they must be constant. For some fanciers, this is possible by growing them in terrariums, which should be given adequate light.

One of the most tolerant, Cattleya trianaei, a short-day plant during the winter months, may be grown on pebble-filled trays. A temperature of about 70 degrees in the daytime and 60 at night is ideal. It should have a weekly feeding during growing periods and correct watering and humidity. This orchid needs light, but if the foliage begins to bleach it is receiving more than it needs.

The principal difference between orchids and other house plants lies in their root system. The orchid root consists of a fine, wirelike center covered with a spongy jacket. The root system serves two functions: to secure the plant to its tree or rock support and to gather moisture and food. The wiry center provides the strength, and the outer cover, which is very absorbent, soaks up available water. This must be done very rapidly for the roots are not in contact with moist soil. To get a drink by this method the

Cymbidium

Moth Orchid

Odontoglossum

Formosana

GREENE

"Some of us orchids are real swingers."

plant must have a large surface area.

To provide the proper environment for your house-grown orchid, break up tree bark and place the smaller pieces in a large pot. For best results use an eight-inch pot for an average-sized plant. This will allow a large root system to form. Excess watering may cause the plant to rot, so reduce watering as necessary to keep the contents moist but not soggy. Experiment a little with your particular plant, and once you find the right balance, try to maintain it.

When watering, pour sufficient water through the pot to completely soak all the fiber. Do not water again until the bark is reasonably dry. Pots should always be allowed to drain after watering. A pebble tray is good to set them on. Water should always be at room temperature. Orchids are light feeders, but you may occasionally give them weak manure tea or compost water as a pick-me-up. You may also add a small amount of leaf mold to the bark from time to time, but be careful not to interfere with the air circulation in the pot, as this is very necessary to the health of the plant.

Many orchids are less fussy about temperature than people think—it should never go below 60 degrees at night but a daytime temperature of 90 will be well tolerated by many species.

What is necessary—if you would have

them bloom—is a high intensity of light. Most orchids like at least five or six hours of sunlight a day and some will enjoy full sun all day. Use caution; orchids can sunburn. Give them time to adjust and they will adapt the pigmentation of their skin to increased light conditions. Check the color of the leaves. If they are a dark green there is insufficient light. Increase the intensity of the light until the leaves turn yellow-green or reddish (depending on the variety you are growing). The intensity should be gradually increased or burn spots may appear—if this happens reduce the light. In this area, orchids are finicky; if the light is not exactly right, they will not bloom.

Many people grow orchids and feel they are no more trouble than other house plants. If you would like to grow several types in the same environment, plan for congenial friends who like the same temperature and humidity—care will be easier and success more probable.

Orchids demand special growing conditions, but their lush, exotic blossoms make them well worth the effort.

Girl Foliage

Rippled Leaf

GREENE

African Violets

Knowing the basic rules for growing African violets is something like having a knowledge of good manners—you must know what's what before you can depart therefrom.

Use a 3-inch pot to set the new plants in—either the common red-clay unglazed flower pot or the glazed containers which are offered with or without a wick for continuous feeding.

If an unglazed pot is used, provide protection on the rim so the leaf stems do not come in direct contact with the pot, which causes stem rot. Coat the rim with paraffin or cover with metal foil. If a glazed pot is used, be sure that drainage is provided at the bottom.

African violets like a loose fertile soil—1 part sharp medium-fine sand, 1 tablespoon bonemeal per quart, 2 parts garden loam, 2 parts leafmold or peat moss and 1 part well-rotted manure, if available. Sift the soil mixture through a ¼-inch screen (a piece of hardware cloth will work fine) to remove any coarse particles.

Use broken crock over the drainage hole in the bottom of the pot to keep it open. This is one of the most important success factors with African violets.

Place the plant in the pot so that the crown is just above the surface. Press the soil about the roots, then thump the pot on the table to further settle the soil. Stand the pot in water until the soil soaks in all it will hold, then set it out to drain.

Observe these precautions:

1. Do not keep plants in direct sunlight, especially in summer. Diffused light as from an east or north window is best, although insufficient light means few flowers.

2. Water should be of room temperature. Always water from the bottom, setting the pot in a saucer. Do not get water on the foliage.

3. Do not allow soil to become soggy; good drainage is important. Check occasionally to be sure the drainage hole is not plugged.

4. For healthy foliage and numerous flowers, maintain a regular feeding program.

5. Watch plants for any indication of insect attack. For mealy bugs, small cottony white spots, touch with a small swab dipped in alcohol. Most other insects can be controlled by dusting with a complete insecticide, especially in the heart of the plant.

Points often hotly disputed are the required temperature and humidity and whether or not the foliage should be cleaned with water or a soft dry brush. After the plants become adjusted to your home, they stand any medium temperature range between 60 and 75 degrees, provided they are not subjected to sudden changes or drafts, or chilled at night.

New flower buds form in the axil of each new leaf, so the more new leaves a plant has, the more flowers it produces. This is one of

African violets bloom almost year-round. Despite their reputation for being hard to raise, they require little special care.

the best reasons for growing them under fluorescent lights. Lights keep the plants growing continuously, putting out new leaves and consequently more flowers. Fluorescent lighting also eliminates the tedious daily task of turning plants to keep them symmetrical.

There are several hundred varieties of African violet. And new ones are being continually introduced. The difference between many of these varieties is so very slight that it's difficult to accurately identify them. Yet this plant has many slight variations in flower size, color, leaf shape, leaf color, leaf margin and leaf marking to entice

you to become an avid collector.

Propagation of African violets sometimes happens by accident. A clump gets too large and you pull off a crown or two. You just can't bear to throw the pretty thing away, so you plant it in a small pot, pat the soil down, water and—you have another plant! This method, which is nearly always successful, is probably the easiest. And you have just done what you should do, potted the new plant quickly without letting the roots dry out—that's the extra plus factor that new plants need.

If one of your friends has a beautiful plant that you admire, it might strain even the most cordial friendship for you to step up and detach a crown, so ask for a leaf. If you have a choice, select a medium-sized leaf, mature but not old, remove it from the parent plant with an inch-long leaf stem.

Put your treasure in a small plastic bag and when you get home, place it in a glass of water, suspended through a slit in a bit of wax paper, cardboard, or aluminum foil. Place the glass where it receives light but not sunshine, and you can confidently expect roots to form in about two weeks to a month. The rooted leaf stem should be planted when the new growth is about an inch long. Or you can plant your leaf in a half and half mixture of sand and vermiculite, or in ordinary gravel, but be sure to keep either quite moist.

African violets may be injured by crown rot, a disease that injures the plant at the soil level, and causes the plant to wilt. Careful watering and good drainage help to prevent this damage. Don't plant too deeply. A plant which has rotted off may sometimes be saved by cutting off the diseased portion and a few of the older leaves and then re-rooting them in sand or water. When new roots have developed, pot the plant in sterilized soil.

Ring spot, characterized by yellowish or white rings or irregular spots noticeable on the upper surface of the leaf, is caused by too much strong light or applying water which is either decidedly warmer or cooler than the plant.

Betsy Begonia

If African violets are presently the most popular plant for indoor culture they may not be for long—begonia bedazzlers are slowly but surely creeping up on them and some day may take first place.

Don't let the delicate beauty of these plants put you off. They are not nearly as complicated as many would have us think. I remember Grandma Putt telling about the time she could no longer withstand temptation, the pictures and descriptions proved too much, so she sat down and ordered a fistful. When they came she had no place to put them but in one of her porch boxes (on the north and in the shade).

She didn't know one cotton-pickin' thing about begonia culture but, after reading the directions, realized that what she was about to do should not happen. No matter, that box was all she had, so in they went. She did provide them with the right soil and then they were on their own.

She was just lucky, I guess, for they bloomed like blossoms were going out of style, right up to fall.

For the tuberous-rooted—these are the frilled and fancy ones that come in almost as many colors as Joseph's coat—the soil should be plentifully enriched with leafmold, compost, decayed manure, humus or peatmoss. It should be coarse and well-drained but moist.

Tuberous begonias may be planted any time from February until spring. They are ready to plant when the buds start to swell at the crown, and should be planted so the pink swellings remain above ground.

Good drainage is a must, so be sure that the bottom of the pot contains plenty of broken crockery. Water sparingly until growth starts, increasing the amount of moisture as the plants develop.

Begonias grow best if kept in a temperature of 65 to 70 degrees and in partial shade.

Grandma Putt's actually grew in daytime temperatures in the nineties and sometimes over a hundred that memorable summer.

In late fall, after the tops die down, allow the plant to dry, then store in a warm place, 50 to 55 degrees.

FIBROUS-ROOTED BEGONIAS

This branch of the begonia family includes a lot of beauties, too, and they are easier to grow than their larger flowering sisters. Their blossoms are not as big but they more than make up for this in abundance.

These begonias are often called wax begonias and may be used either for pot culture or as bedding plants. Most of these grow to an average height of about 12 inches, though the angel-wing begonia sometimes grows 12 feet tall.

The angel-wing begonia has evergreen leaves and great bundles of cerise-colored flowers. It is a climber and is very pretty grown on wires fixed to the greenhouse roof. It can be kept within bounds by taking cuttings from it each spring. The leaves resemble wings.

Smaller wax begonias also have evergreen leaves. They are roundish and the plants bear clusters of pink, white, red or dark crimson flowers. Though they bloom almost continuously, the greatest profusion of blossoms are produced during the summer.

Rex begonias are practical for people who work or live in apartments. These beauties have short rhizomes or root-stocks, and from these arise long-stalked, ovate, wrinkled leaves averaging about six inches in diameter.

With these boy-types, the leafstalks, veins, and, in some varieties, the upper surfaces of the leaves, are covered with fine hairs. The beautifully marked leaves may be silver and green, light and dark green, red and green, purple and green and on and on. One of the most striking, begonia Massoniana (Iron Cross), has green leaves distinctly marked with radiating bands of chocolate brown.

Rex needs warmth (a minimum temperature of from 50 to 55 degrees), and moisture. His soil requirements are much the same as other types—the best potting compost consists of loam and leaf mold in equal parts along with coarse sand and rotted manure. Add some charcoal to keep the mixture "sweet." Water well in summer, but during the winter months only when the soil becomes dry. Propagation is easily accomplished by division or by leaf cuttings.

"You're tops, Pineapple. Let's put down roots together."

Have Your House Plants and Eat Them Too

A number of house plants are very attractive, easily grown and, though humble in origin, mix well with tropicals. I am referring to such prosaic things as sweet potatoes, carrots, beets and rutabagas, all of which produce interesting foliage.

Growing a sweet potato is utter simplicity.

You can even use a pickle jar for the container. Since sweet potatoes are often treated with a material to retard sprouting, use a homegrown one or find one that shows some signs of life.

If you are in any doubt about which end to insert in the jar, lay the potato on a moist bed of peat or sphagnum moss and leave it in a warm place for a few days. When growth starts, insert the potato in the jar with its lower end just touching the water. (A lump of charcoal in the water will help to keep it sweet). As water evaporates, add more.

A mass of roots will soon form inside the jar and sprouts will appear all over the upper part of the potato. These sprouts may grow several feet long, especially if you will pinch back all but two or three of the strongest.

Several sweet potatoes placed in a bowl can make a very attractive centerpiece for your table. Beet roots may be grown in the same way as sweet potatoes.

To grow a carrot or rutabaga top, cut it about three inches from the top. Choose a low bowl, deep enough so the top can stand upright when it is covered with pebbles, leaving about ¼ to ½ inch exposed. Cover the pebbles with water, and add water as it evaporates. You will get an abundance of pretty fern-like foliage from the carrot and interesting leaves from the rutabaga.

Narcissus

Agapanthus

Gloxinia

Freesia

Bella Bulb

Grandma Putt always said that Mother Nature expressly designed bulbs for the impatient gardener who just couldn't wait for spring. Forcing bulbs to bloom indoors can be just as much fun as any other form of gardening. Approached in the right way, it need not be messy or difficult. As with most other things, getting it all together before you start will make the whole procedure go more smoothly.

The spring-flowering bulbs, paperwhites, crocuses, grape hyacinths, scillas, chionodoxas, daffodils, hyacinths, snowdrops and the single early and early double tulips can all be forced into flower.

The best containers are called "bulb pans." They are clay pots which are wide at the top and shallower than standard pots. There are all sorts of variations, depending on what you plan to grow. Azalea pots, for instance, are deeper than bulb pans but not so deep as standard pots.

The mechanical condition of the soil is much more important than its fertility, because the bulb contains enough stored food within itself to bring forth a good flower. A good general potting mixture consists of equal parts of top soil, humus and sand. Add a little plant food or well-decayed manure if you like. In a large container, mix all the ingredients thoroughly so it is well pulverized.

In choosing your bulbs, select only those marked suitable for indoor forcing. Ten days to three weeks is the longest you can reasonably expect your bulbs to stay in flower. Hardy bulbs bloom naturally outside during the cool and even frosty days of late winter and early spring. Forcing them indoors does not mean using a high temperature.

Provide drainage in the bottom of the pot with pieces of broken crock. Fill the pot about half full and place the bulbs on top of the soil. Plant several to a container, so they almost touch each other. Fill in around the bulbs but leave the tips uncovered. The tips should be just seen above the surface of the soil, and the soil should be an inch below the rim of the pot to allow for watering.

After potting the bulbs mark them as to color and variety with labeling sticks. Give them a thorough watering. The best way is to stand the pots in a pan of water, letting it seep upward until the surface soil is completely moistened. Then set them where they can drain.

After the bulbs are potted, they are ready for a period of cold and darkness. This time of cold and darkness enables them to develop a strong root system before their top growth starts. Most bulbs need a minimum of ten to twelve weeks of the cold and dark treatment before you can safely bring them in.

Where will you put the bulbs in the meantime? Most home gardeners dig a trench 12 to 15 inches deep, 18 inches wide, and long enough to hold the number of pots they plan to put in it. The trench should be dug in a well-drained part of the garden where there is no danger of water collecting in the bottom. Place a four-inch layer of cinders or coarse gravel in the bottom, to help the drainage.

Set the pots in the trench with the rims touching. Pack damp compost or peat moss around the pots and three inches deep over them. Just before freezing, place a heavy layer of old hay or straw over the peat moss. Weight this down with boards or evergreen branches. This prevents the pots from being frozen too solidly in the peat moss, making removal difficult. After ten or twelve weeks, examine some of the pots. If you see roots growing out of the drainage hole, it's time to take a few of them inside.

Put them in a cool, light, but not sunny, place—a cellar or a north room. Check the moisture of the pot soil; it must never be allowed to dry out completely. To water, set the pots in a partially filled basin and let the soil soak up the water from the bottom.

Once the leaf growth is well up, place the pots in a moderately warm, sunny window. The night temperature should never be higher than 60 degrees.

When they are in the flower and bud stage, all bulbs need daily watering. The cooler the room, the longer bulb flowers will last, so remove them from direct sunlight once the flowers start to open. At night, place the pots in a room where the temperature ranges between 40 and 50 degrees to help prolong the life of the flowers.

After blooming, remove the faded flowers but do not reduce watering. Wait until the foliage shows signs of maturing. Store the pots temporarily, and as soon as the ground can be dug, put the hardy bulbs out in the garden to grow on for a year and have a chance to recover their vitality.

When the foliage on the half-hardy and tender bulbs dies, they should be rested completely. Allow the bulbs and corms to remain in their pots or remove and dry them completely. If they remain in their pots, they should have a small amount of moisture, best provided by setting the pots in a cool, damp place.

Water Babies

There are special glasses made for the express purpose of growing hyacinth bulbs in water. If possible, use rainwater and fill the glass almost to the base of the bulb. A few pieces of charcoal help keep the water sweet. Place the glasses in a cool, dark room until the growth is about 3 inches high, then move them to a place of honor.

Paperwhite narcissuses are the easiest bulbs to force, and the snowy flowers are delightfully fragrant. They need not be planted in soil, and they do not need a resting period in the dark. Select shallow containers, just deep enough to hold enough pebbles or small stones so the bulbs, when set in place on top of these, will have at least two inches of space below for the roots.

After placing the stones in the container, set the paperwhites on them three or four inches apart. Add water at room temperature, bringing the level up to within ½ inch

Hyacinths may be grown in special glasses or plastic pots designed to support the bulb.

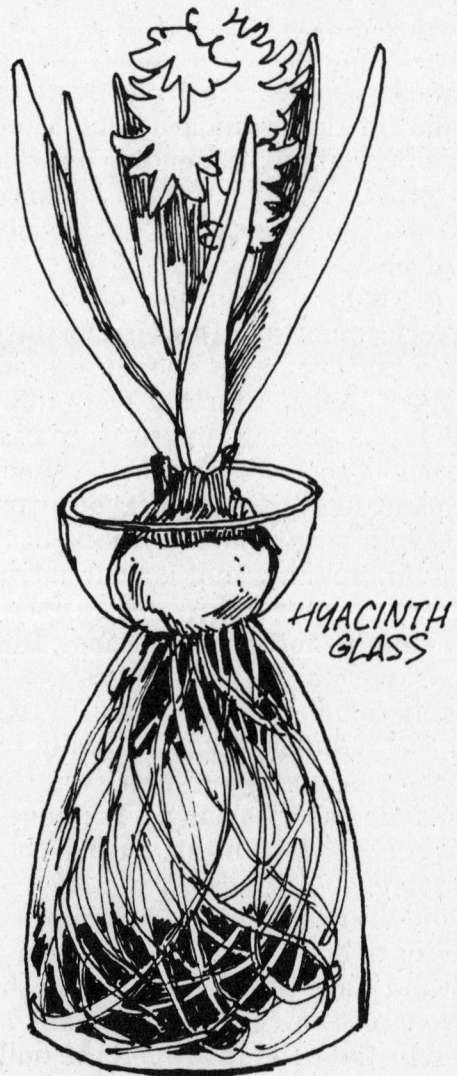

HYACINTH GLASS

above the bottom of the bulbs. As the water evaporates, add enough to keep the level constant. Keep the container in a sunny window.

Remove the pan from the sun as soon as the buds start to open. It is difficult to get paperwhites to bloom successfully for another season; the best thing to do is to discard them completely after blossoming.

SUMMER FLOWERING BULBS

Many summer flowering bulbs can also be grown as pot plants, useful indoors or pretty to brighten up the patio.

Achimenes grow 8 to 12 inches high and bloom in summer. The abundantly produced flowers come in almost every color and include both singles and doubles.

Plant the tubers in 4-inch pots in early spring. Use a mixture of equal parts of peat moss, sand and garden soil. Grow the plants in a lightly shaded area away from direct sunlight.

Water and fertilize the plants at monthly intervals throughout the growing season. Use a mixture of one teaspoon of 20-20-20 soluble fertilizer per gallon of water.

The foliage dies down in the fall. Take them up, with the soil still clinging to them, and allow to dry, then store them in a cool, dry area at a minimum of 50 degrees. In the spring, wash the soil from the rhizomes and start the growing cycle again.

I have grown achimenes, sometimes called magic flowers, for many years and, while they are all easy to grow, I have the best results with Purple King. As soon as the weather settles in late spring, I fill my porch boxes with these tubers. Here they receive the north light but no direct sunshine. They make such a spectacle of themselves all summer long that passers-by often come trotting up my front walk to get a better look at "those huge African violets!" Few leave, even complete strangers, without a small rooted piece of tuber. I simply can't bear the pleading look in their eyes!

Caladiums have long been popular for their large, multi-colored leaves.

Caladiums, like Rex begonias, are grown for their colorful leaves. These natives of Brazil are heat-loving tender bulbs.

They have heart, or arrow-shaped leaves, in almost limitless variations of pink, white and red. These are accented with green or red veinings in intricate patterns. Ordinary tall varieties grow up to 18 inches, but dwarf varieties attain a height of only 9 inches.

Colocasia, or elephant's ear, is also a caladium. The heart-shaped leaves of this species are huge, measuring up to 2 feet in length. Elephant's ear plants, sometimes

grown in tubs, will grow 6 feet or more tall.

Despite their delicate appearance, rainbow-hued caladiums are easy to grow. Bulbs can be started indoors any time from late February through April. They need 6 to 8 weeks to develop clumps of several strong leaves. The potting mix should be about half and half peat moss and coarse sand. Cover the planted tubers with a one-inch layer of peat moss.

Water the tubers often enough to keep the soil mixture damp. Roots grow from the top of the tubers; they must be kept moist and covered with peat moss. Keep the room temperature no lower than 70 degrees. Tubers often rot in cool soil.

As soon as roots develop, replant the tubers, putting them in 6-inch pots. Use a mixture of equal parts garden soil and peat moss. Grow the plants in a lightly shaded area, never in direct sunlight, as the leaves burn easily. Try to balance the light and shade to get the most color in the leaves. When plants are grown in deep shade, the leaves will have more green coloring and less pink or red.

Water and fertilize caladium at least once every week. Fertilize with a mixture of one teaspoon of 20-20-20 soluble fertilizer to a gallon of water.

ISMENE

Ismene is a lovely Peruvian daffodil which grows 2 feet high and produces large, funnel-shaped, white flowers striped with green.

Plant the tubers close together in a flat from January to mid-May. Pot, transplant and treat the same as caladiums.

AMARYLLISES

Amaryllis (hippeastrum), grows to about 3 feet tall. The handsome flowers—large and funnel-shaped—are rose, blush or white and are borne on stems 18 inches high.

Plant the bulbs in May with the upper third of the bulb exposed. Blooms will be bigger and better if the bulb is pot-bound.

Amaryllis does not like to be disturbed once it has become established, so repot only when absolutely necessary.

From the time the bulb is potted until growth begins, water very little. Place the pot in a dim light and leave until new growth appears. When new growth starts, increase the moisture and bring the pot to full light.

When the large bud appears, give weekly feedings of manure tea or liquid fertilizer until the buds start to show color.

After blooming, cut off the flower stalk and gradually reduce watering until the foliage dries off, then rest the bulbs in their pots turned on their sides.

The next year, hose some of the soil out of

the top of the pot, and replace it with fresh soil. When new growth appears, move the plant into light and increase watering. You should have more and larger blossoms than the year before.

POTTED LILIES

Easter lilies are not the only lilies that can be grown in pots. Mid-Century Hybrids also make lovely potted plants.

These lilies have a color range that is pure enchantment—Destiny, a lemon-yellow; Croesus, golden-orange; Joan Evans and Harmony, rich orange; Cinnabar and Tabasco, deep maroon-red; Enchantment, blazing orange; and an outward-facing type, Prosperity, which is lemon-yellow.

Use a loose, porous soil, with an inch of gravel placed in the bottom of the pot. A soil mix of 2 parts sandy loam, 2 parts leafmold (or peat) and 1 part sand is ideal.

Place all varieties (except Prosperity), in a temperature of 60 degrees during the day and 55 degrees at night. Prosperity should be placed in a temperature of 40 to 50 degrees until roots are established, then placed in a higher temperature.

When growth has been established and roots are forming, feed with nitrogen. Ten days later, feed again. Wait another ten days and feed with a complete fertilizer and continue until buds appear.

Moisture is important and should be uniform. Too much water will cause root rot.

All bulbs will bloom, but the larger the bulb, the more buds you will have.

LYCORIS

This lovely plant, also called "Spider Lily," has beautiful delicate flowers that come in several colors. Lycoris grows 15 to 18 inches tall, depending on season and variety. Plant the bulbs in 5- or 6-inch pots in a mixture of equal parts of garden soil, peat moss and sand. Water and fertilize the plants at weekly intervals. Use a light ring of 5-10-15 or 10-6-4 around each plant.

A pot of blooming lilies will add a touch of drama to any decor.

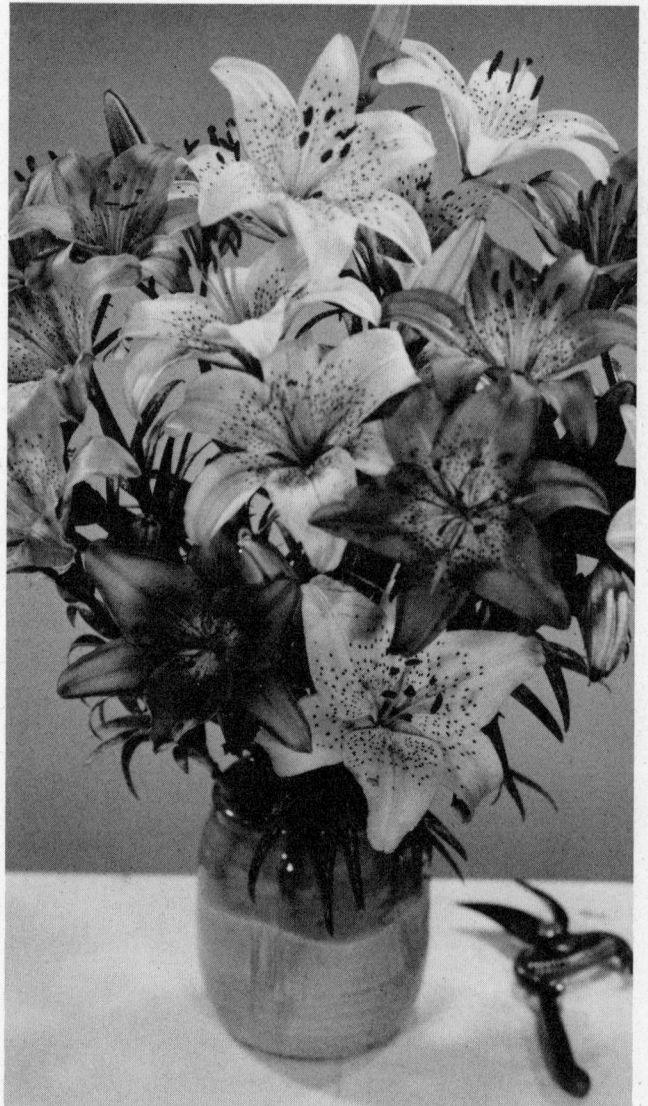

TUBEROSES

Tuberose (polianthes), grows to about 2 feet high and blooms in late fall. Its waxy, white, double flowers are very fragrant. Plant the tubers in 5- to 6-inch pots in a mixture of equal parts of garden soil, peat moss and sand. Water plants every day and fertilize every other week.

Tubers should be taken from the pots in the fall and stored.

DISPLAYING YOUR PLANTS

The shades and textures of green leaves are a decorating plus in any room. Grouping plants can add to their effectiveness. Here are a couple of ideas for showing off your good-looking plants.

Make a plant ladder by painting an ordinary ladder an accent color and widening a few of the rungs with wood, if necessary, to accommodate your larger plants. You might want to hang some plants from the higher rungs.

A beautiful setting for plants can be made easily by arranging glazed ceramic tiles in a pattern of your choosing on the floor. You can move the tiles around to suit your fancy since they are not attached permanently.

For a double harvest of beauty and good eating, try raising a few vegetables on your patio or window sill.

Kitchen Table House Plants

Mini-gardening with vegetables, fruit trees and herbs can be fascinating. You can grow them in your greenhouse, under fluorescent lights, or in a sunny window. Though the type and kind are somewhat more limited than outdoor culture permits, the satisfaction may be just as great. And the hybridists are on our side. They've been busy for a long time creating new types of old favorites that are just as delicious but require smaller space to grow.

The basic materials needed for a mini-gar-den are containers, soil (either garden loam or synthetic) and seeds.

As with house plants, vegetables have preferences, but garden loam will grow most things. Be sure to mix in plenty of organic material so the potting soil will have good water-holding capacity, aeration and drainage.

If you live in an apartment or mobile home, you may not be able to get this type of soil. So what do you do? You buy a ready-to-use soil substitute, or synthetic soil, prepared from a mixture of horticultural vermiculite, peat moss, and fertilizer. This has several advantages over soil. It is free of plant disease organisms and weed seeds; it holds moisture and plant nutrients well; and it is very lightweight and portable.

Prepare your own soil substitute from horticultural grade vermiculite, peat moss, limestone, superphosphate, and 5-10-5 fertilizer. To one bushel each of vermiculite and shredded peat moss, add 14 ounces of ground limestone (preferably dolomitic), 4 ounces of 29 percent superphosphate, and 8 ounces of 5-10-5 fertilizer. If the material is very dry, add a little water to it to reduce the dust, then mix well.

There are many varieties of seeds for each plant. Miniature vegetable varieties are best for mini-gardens. Miniature varieties now available include cabbage, cantaloupe, carrot, cucumber, eggplant, tomato, onion, sweet corn, head lettuce, peas, watermelon and, if you are quite adventurous, mushroom spawn. Many types of standard size vegetables, such as lettuce, can be grown indoors. And there are many varieties of ornamental peppers suitable for seasoning, which also make pretty house plants.

Vegetable plants grow best in full sunlight. Leafy vegetables can stand more shade than root vegetables and root vegetables can stand more shade than vegetable fruit plants (cucumbers, peppers, tomatoes), which do very poorly in the shade.

Vegetables need a water supply equal to about one inch of rain every week during the growing season. Since you are gardening in containers instead of garden plot, you can easily control moisture. Water each time the soil becomes dry down to a depth of one-eighth inch, but don't overdo it. Overwatering slowly kills your plants.

If you use a sprinkler can, do not water so late in the evening that the leaves of plants stay wet at night. Wet leaves encourage plant diseases. It is important to fill the bottom of your plant containers with gravel or similar material. This allows for good drainage. If your soil becomes waterlogged the plants will die from lack of oxygen.

INSECTS AND DISEASES

Vegetables grown in mini-gardens are as susceptible to attack by insects and diseases as those grown in a garden plot. This is especially true if they are grown near other plants. But remember these plants are going to be eaten, so do not use anything on them that could prove detrimental later on. Try some of the organic remedies before the problem gets a stranglehold.

DECORATE WITH VEGETABLES

With a little imagination, your indoor vegetables can be as attractive as your favorite house-plant "regulars." To keep vegetables growing vigorously, place them in your sunniest window or on a sunny corner of your balcony or patio. You might even plant some in a windowbox.

A cherry tomato plant cascading out of a hanging basket would look lovely in a bright kitchen window. Occasionally open the window and let the wind blow across your tomato plant; if you don't, the blossoms won't be pollinated and the plant won't set fruit.

Maybe you'd like to fill a window box (indoors or out) with different kinds of lettuce. The different textures and colors of the leaves will make this planting as ornamental as it is delicious. When the lettuce goes to seed, you can replace it with cucumbers, cherry tomatoes or peppers. Some of the hot red or yellow peppers would make a zesty and colorful addition.

TOMATOES

LETTUCE

Orange

GREENE

Lemon

Avocado

A Fruitful Hobby

The variety and types of fruits that can be grown indoors is amazing. Gardeners everywhere have discovered that it is not only possible but often easy to grow warm-climate plants in the north. Of course the answer is tub culture, but, while vegetables may be grown in substitute soil, I do not recommend this for small trees. Grow these in soil that is rich in humus. They may be placed outdoors in the summer, but you should also provide a suitable environment for them to thrive in during the winter months.

Growing fruit trees indoors is nothing new—in fact, it was quite the thing a century or two ago when just about every wealthy estate in Europe boasted an "orangery." Here, not only oranges but many other tropical plants were grown. These, often huge in size, were taken outdoors in summer and used as ornamentals in the estate gardens, but were stored and displayed in winter in ornate glass structures. Today, interest in tub culture is again reviving, for fruits—especially citrus trees—are exceptionally beautiful and often intensely fragrant.

The best tubs are wooden and the best woods are cedar, cypress, oak or redwood. With good provision for drainage, you can reasonably expect to have such a planter last at least 10 years and some woods will last even longer. If they are put together with removable bolts, disassembling them for root pruning will be a fairly simple matter. They should also have wood or metal handles for easier movability.

Be sure to place drainage material in the bottom of the tub before putting in the soil. Since most of the plants you will grow will be tropicals, this should be well-enriched with good, humusy material that is loose, porous and well-balanced in plant nutrients. If you

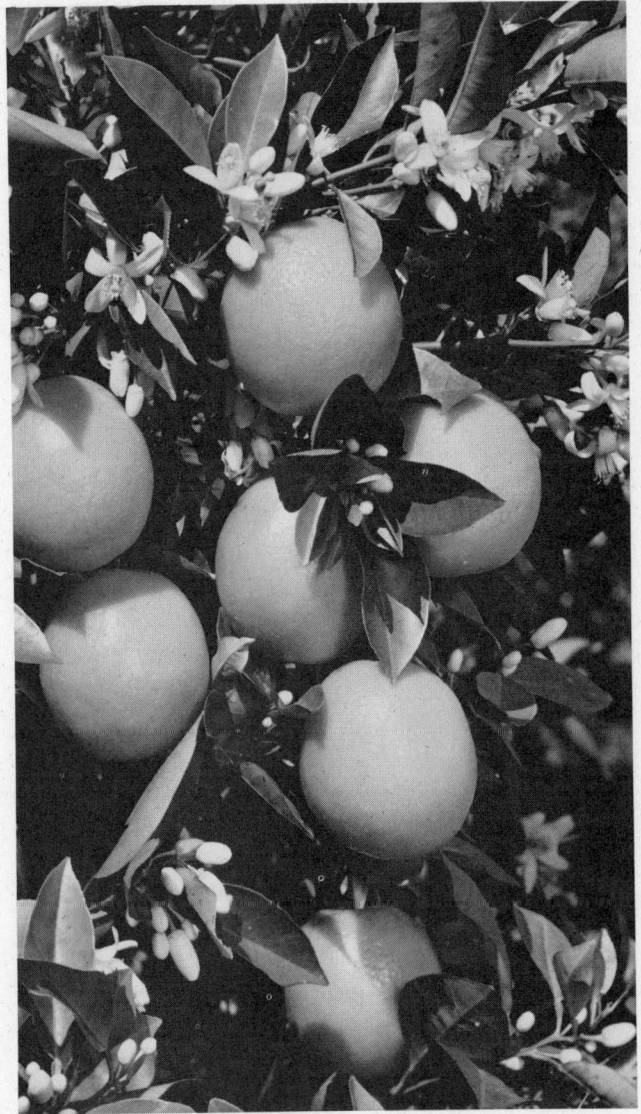

are in any doubt, have the soil tested just as you would for an outdoor garden. You may find that the addition of phosphate rock, finely ground potash or bone meal may be needed when you make up the potting mixture.

Remember that fruit trees, like other potted plants, cannot reach out with their roots you must bring what they need to them. Manure tea, compost water tea, and diluted fish emulsion are all good to use as liquid fertilizers. Used periodically, they will keep the plants healthy and stimulate growth.

Next to soil, the most important factor is light. Fruiting plants need all they can get. You will get some fruit in a lightly shaded location, but plants will bear far more heavily in full sun.

Temperature is also important, and the best growing climate ranges from 65 to 75 degrees with cooler temperatures at night down to about 55 or 60 degrees. This is important because trees, like other plants, need to rest at night, which enables them to mature the growth they have made during the day.

Do your watering with care. No house plant should be allowed to suffer from lack of moisture, but overwatering can be just as bad as underwatering. When you water, water deeply, then let the plant remain dry for a while. Avoid a dry atmosphere. Citrus plants prefer humid conditions. Even indoors these conditions can be provided by placing the pot in a container half filled with coarse sand or fine gravel; keep this material wet at all times. The evaporation of the water from the sand or gravel humidifies the plants.

Place the plants outdoors during the summer months if you live in a cold climate. When they bloom outdoors, bees and other insects aid in pollinating the blossoms. Plants that are grown indoors exclusively should be lightly shaken each day they are in bloom in order to distribute the pollen and insure a set of fruit. Improper pollination and a too-dry atmosphere are often the causes of fruit not setting on plants that bloom indoors. However, over-fertilization and over-watering can

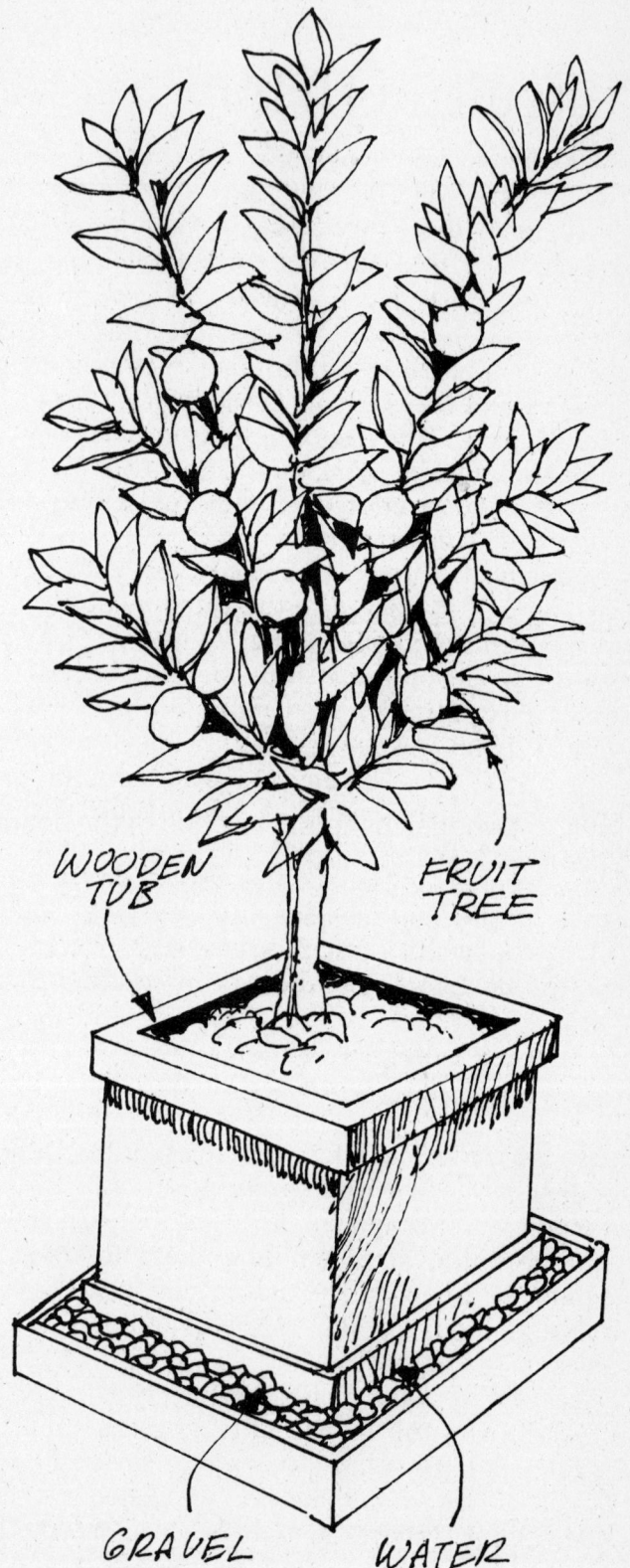

WOODEN TUB

FRUIT TREE

GRAVEL   WATER

also cause a failure of the plants to bear fruit.

To prevent scale or other insects from attacking the plant wash the leaves and stems at least once every two months in lukewarm water which contains a small amount of soap. This also gets rid of dust which may clog the breathing pores of the leaves.

After the bath in sudsy water, rinse the plant in cool, not cold, clear water and allow the foliage to dry before placing the plant in direct sunlight.

WOODEN TUB

Large wooden tubs are often quite expensive. But you can build a sturdy, attractive tub yourself for very little money. One of the easiest ways to do so is to nail together nine courses of thick wooden boards. The ends of the boards should alternate at the corners. The bottom should be made of marine plywood and mounted on two boards. If you use a wood other than redwood, apply a preservative to every piece before you start building. If you like, you can stain the tub a soft, natural color when you finish.

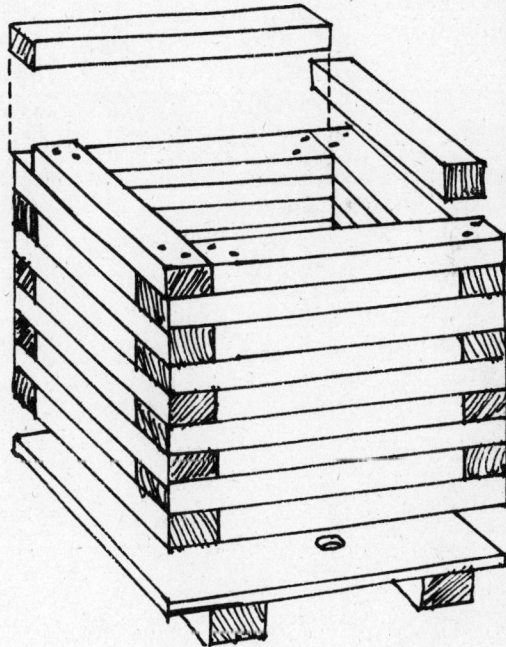

Sage

Purple Basil

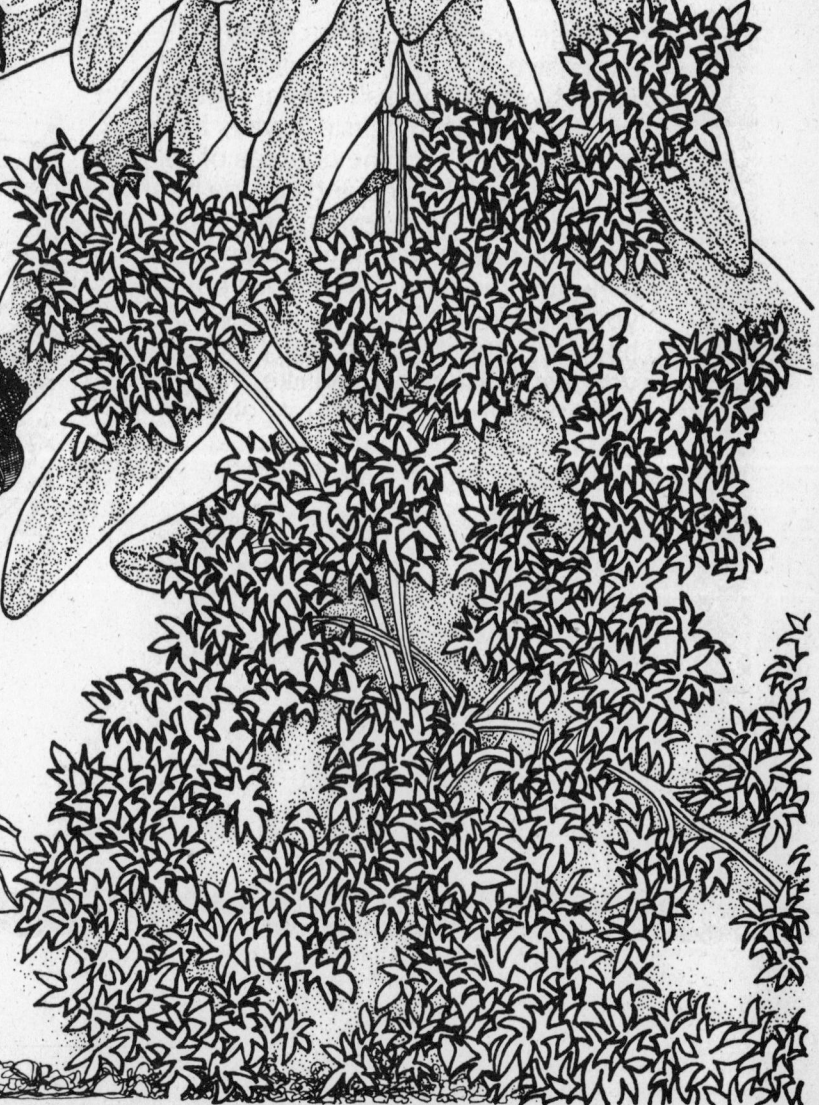

Parsley

Henrietta Herb

A strawberry jar doesn't have to be used for strawberries—it is an almost perfect container for a large variety of herbs. You can have a small kitchen garden in one of these pretty containers. What you will plant in it is entirely up to you as it may be used for either annuals or perennials—or both.

As with many other things there's a trick to filling it correctly. Secure a length of plastic pipe, about one inch smaller than the jar's opening and long enough to be inserted the full depth of the jar.

Using a sharp instrument (a nail will do), pierce holes in the pipe at intervals about two or three inches apart, so that water can seep out at all levels into the soil. Keep the opening covered with a bit of masking tape until the soil is in place.

Herbs do not like especially rich soil, so fill the jar with a mixture of sandy loam. Start filling the plants in from the bottom, setting each one in place as you go and continuing up the sides. Tamp the soil down carefully and be sure the roots are well covered. When you reach the top, leave an inch or so of the pipe uncovered so soil will not fall into it. Take off the masking tape and water the jar thoroughly so there will be no air pockets around the roots of any of the plants.

Rose geranium or moss-curled parsley are particularly pretty for setting at the top of the jar. You may even want to plant such a jar entirely with scented geraniums which include rose, nutmeg, lemon, peppermint and apple. Other possibilities are annuals such as dill, basil, chervil, anise and summer savory.

If you plant the jar with annuals, be sure to keep the soil moist until germination takes place. Slipping a large plastic cover over the jar for a day or two prevents drying out and converts the jar into a miniature greenhouse. Sometimes herb seeds are slow to germinate so be patient—parsley, especially, takes time. If you do secure a good stand, thin the plants to just a few in each opening—crowded plants will be spindly.

Herbs need sunshine. A sunny window will be just fine, but you must remember to turn the jar at regular intervals so all the plants will receive the sun in turn.

Herbs do not seem to grow as tall indoors as they do in the garden, especially if you pot them young. They should be given a chance to adjust and given protection from wind and excessive heat. Them, too, you will use your kitchen herbs, cutting them regularly for soups, salads and other seasonings, and this will help to control their height.

To Love and Cherish

This is the chapter that usually bears a depressing label like "Pests and Diseases" or "Trouble," and maybe that's what I should call it. Somehow, I can't. Of course plants, like people, do get sick and insects do sometimes trouble them, but often their distress is not caused for either of these reasons.

The plain truth is that house plants were probably the first sufferers from environmental pollution. Consider the fact that they come from all corners of the world, many of the most beautiful from the tropics. And we, in our clumsy, well-meaning way, often try to grow them under conditions so unsuitable as to damage their health, stunt their growth, or even kill them.

A plant may be unhealthy for several different reasons. There may be a fungus, virus or bacterium which is causing either local or general infection. An insect or pest of some sort, such as a snail or a slug, may be gnawing or chewing away at its vitals. Or it may be suffering from a physiogenic disease, which simply means that we have not provided it with the correct environment. An atmosphere which is either too hot or too dry, too much or too little light, too much or too little water—or even a cold draft blowing on its leaves—any of these conditions can cause problems. Or maybe we unthinkingly and rudely shocked it by pouring ice-cold water on it.

Here another factor enters. Strong, healthy plants, like strong, healthy people, are less prone to disease—and less likely to be attacked by insects. Plants in pots are already at a disadvantage in their fight for life, struggling to live in an unnatural existence.

If you are at all in doubt about the needs of a particular plant, look it up in a good gardening encyclopedia—or find a book about your specialty. Don't guess—know!

Make sure the soil mixture you are using is the right one. Remember that a pot is a very limited area.

This lush fern is undoubtedly loved and cherished by its fortunate owner.

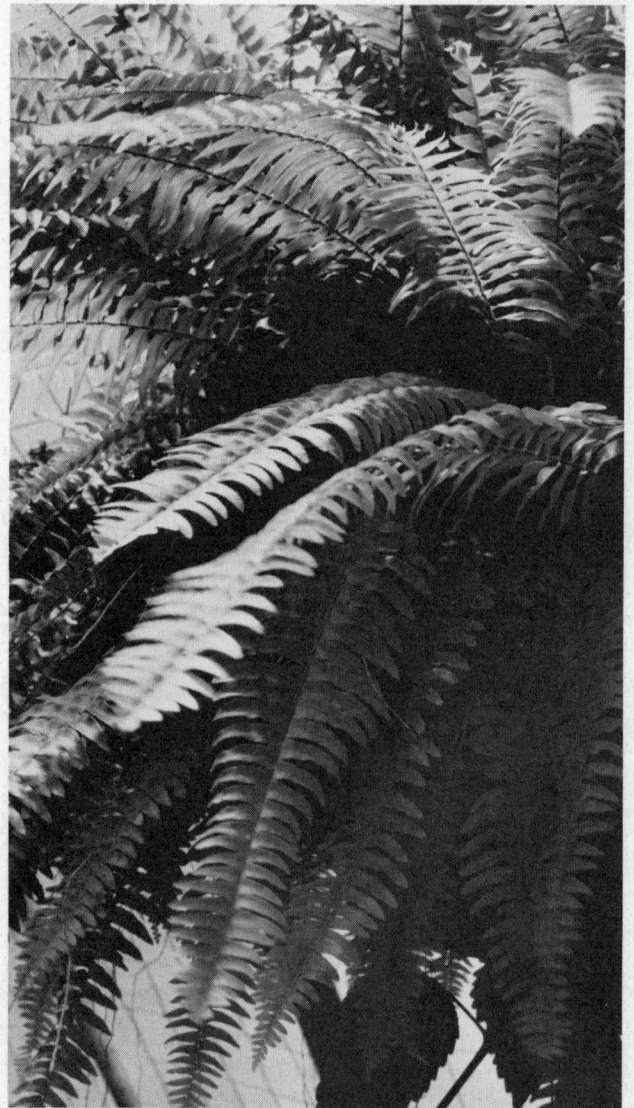

And so are these bright-leaved coleus. To keep your plants this healthy and beautiful, water early in the morning with room-temperature water.

An Early Morning Drink

Water your plants in the morning with water that is at room temperature. Put it on the soil and not on the plants. Begin feeding with the right fertilizer at the proper time. House plants respond to spring just as outdoor plants do. When they begin to make new growth and come into bud and flower, they are working very hard and they need more food.

It is possible that our attitude toward plants is the true source of that gardening accolade, the "green thumb." We all know people who "can get anything to grow." Such people are not always those that we, in our ignorance, consider "beautiful." They may be an elderly farmer, a withered grandmother, even a child. But the gift is theirs, even though their knowledge of the scientific principles of plant growth may be nonexistent. The true gardener, just like the creative artist, develops an instinctive identification with his plants.

What, then, do you need to become an effective healer? First of all, you must cultivate your powers of observation—really see what you are looking at. Watch especially for changes in the leaves. Do they drop? Is there a change in color? Is there something on them that wasn't there yesterday?

Grandma Putt's Old-Time Remedies

We need not rely wholly on chemicals to combat many pests and diseases. There are still natural remedies that can be used. They are just as effective today as when Grandma Putt raised house plants in the bay window of her living or dining room.

Spider mites, for instance, are the bane of many gardeners lives. If you're plagued with these pests, try buttermilk and wheat flour—1/2 cup buttermilk and 4 cups wheat flour. Mix well and add 5 gallons of water.

This destroys most of the mites and the mite eggs as well.

A spray made with one part skimmed milk to nine parts of water is good against most

diseases. It is particularly good for tomatoes. Azaleas like an acid soil, so Grandma Putt occasionally added two table-spoons of vinegar to a quart of water, then watered hers. She also believed that cuttings rooted better in an acid soil, so she added vinegar to the beds where cuttings were rooted. Vinegar added to the water in which cut flowers are kept also helps prevent spoilage.

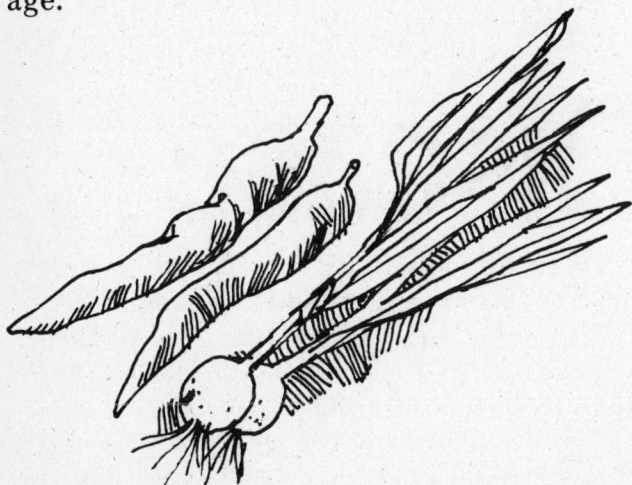

Hot pepper and garlic, crushed, steeped, and mixed with water, makes a potent spray that discourages many insects and gives the rest a good case of heartburn.

A soap and water bath is still one of the best ways to keep indoor plants healthy. Besides cleanliness, the soap is particularly useful against soft-bodied pests such as aphids.

If you smoke, use plenty of soap to wash your hands before touching your plants. Many, such as petunias, peppers, eggplants and tomatoes, are susceptible to tobacco mosaic virus, which may be on your hands.

It is not easy, even for an experienced gardener, to accurately diagnose what is troubling a plant. If a plant has been growing vigorously and it begins to develop any of the symptoms we've talked about, treatment is indicated as quickly as possible. Don't let the infestation or disease get a strong hold and spread before taking remedial measures.

On the other hand, don't think that you must save every plant—or that you are a failure as a green thumber if you do not. Don't feel guilty if you must discard some plants. Discretion is still often the better part of valor. Throwing away a badly diseased plant may save many others from the same fate. Not even a gardening "godfather" could cure everything!

Then, too, there are some plants that just never seem to have gotten a good start in life. Everyone who has raised seedlings has observed this—there are always big, husky fellows and "runts". Sometimes the "little guys" never really catch up. It is very often the weak and spindly ones that are attacked first, and, with insufficient strength to fight, they die. By that time the disease or pest has grown stronger and moved on to stronger, healthier plants. Keep your eyes open. With insects, disease, or environmental problems, "Eternal vigilance is still the price of freedom"—from the heartbreak of losing a beloved plant friend.

Disease

Diseases caused by fungi and bacterial organisms are infrequent among plants grown in homes. The low humidity in homes usually harms such disease organisms more than it does house plants. But if you notice spots and speckles in the leaves, indicative of leaf diseases, apply a garden fungicide.

Numerous soil-borne disease organisms are capable of causing stem, crown and root rots. Stem rots cause portions of the stem to become discolored and soft and to eventually die. The best treatment is prompt surgery. Cut away all diseased tissue, dust cut surfaces with powdered sulfur, and keep the plants somewhat dry. Try to avoid wetting stems and foliage when stem rot is prevalent.

Even robust, healthy plants like these primroses have an occasional bout with disease, but with a little help from you, they'll soon be on the road to recovery.

ROOT ROT

Root rot diseases are caused by various fungus organisms and are more serious than either stem or crown rot. All soils in which flowers or vegetables have been recently grown contain some fungi. The damage from root rot is aggravated by overwatering, crowding of plants and poor drainage. The most effective control is treating the potting soil with heat to kill the soil-borne organisms before planting or potting.

BLIGHT

Blight often infects begonias. A grayish mold appears on the leaves and flowers. Avoid wetting the leaves and remove and destroy all infected parts.

LEAF DROP

Leaf drop infects begonias and poinsettias. In begonias leaf drop may be caused by wet, heavy soil, hot, dry air or drafts. Put in a cool room that has a high humidity and be sure the soil is porous. Leaf drop in poinsettias is usually caused by too warm temperatures. Move to a cooler room.

CHLOROSIS

Chlorosis is characterized by yellow, irregular mottling on the leaves. It is caused by too much strong light or wetting the leaves. It infects African violets, aspidistras, azaleas, and gardenias. Treat by moving to a shaded area.

LEAF SPOT

Leaf spot is characterized by white spots on the leaves, brown margins on leaf blades and stalks, or pale spots on the leaves. Remove and burn all infected leaves. Control by sprinkling the plants and placing them further apart so they can have better circulation.

RED FIRE

Red fire disease infects amaryllis. Look for red spots on the leaves, flowers and bulb scales. Flower stalks and foliage will look bent and deformed. Remove and burn all infected parts.

POWDERY MILDEW

Powdery mildew is a fungus disease characterized by a grayish white, powdery, or mealy covering on stem and leaves. It infects kalanchoes, African violets, begonias, primroses and numerous other house plants. It usually occurs when the atmosphere is humid and stagnant. Good air circulation is a preventive. Dusting with sulfur cures the disease.

BLACK LEG

Black leg, which infects coleus and geraniums, causes plants to wilt and sometimes die. It is best to destroy all infected plants.

The best way to keep an impressive plant like this free of insects is to keep it strong and vigorous.

Insect Enemies

You would think that sheltered indoors and protected as house plants are, they would be free from insects. But there numerous insects that attack them. Be particularly careful about new plants brought into the house. Keep them separate from your other plants for a week or two. Even cut flowers may be carriers of insects or diseases.

Insects may also enter through open windows or doors and many times are brought into a home on clothing. Once in, the tiny insects multiply very rapidly and infest a number of plants. If they escape early detection and become established, control is much more difficult, and considerably more plant damage occurs. The most common damage is caused by sucking insects. The loss of juices interferes with normal growth, development and flowering.

Examine the underside of the leaves of house plants every week or two and carefully examine the stems. Insects are much easier to detect than diseases. But detection is not enough; it is also important to identify the insect so the proper chemical control measure may be applied. Use stomach poison for chewing insects. Sucking insects avoid stomach poisons, so contact spray is necessary for their control.

If spraying, be sure to dampen the underside of each leaf. Repeat this treatment two or three times at weekly intervals. A Malathion spray or an aerosol house plant bomb (not household), is also effective. In using any spray bomb, be sure to hold it at least eighteen inches from the plant. To prevent infestations of red spider mites, spray once a week. Use sufficient force to break the webs and wash away the mites, but do not damage the foilage.

APHIDS

Aphids are small, green, grey, black, or red insects usually found clustered on new growth, buds, or the underside of leaves. Examination of stems and leaves easily reveals the presence of these sneaky insects. They are oval and fringed with short white filaments.

Spray or dip the plant in a solution of nicotine sulfate and soak every few days until control is complete. Each aphid must be thoroughly wetted to cause its death. It is difficult to reach those hidden in the folds of immature leaves. Dipping the aboveground portions of plants in a spray material is best because all portions of the plant come into contact with the chemical. Malathion is also useful against aphids.

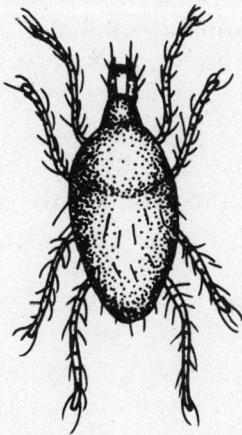

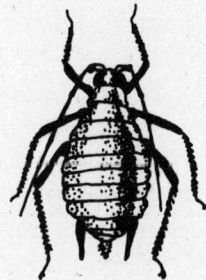

RED SPIDER MITES

Red spider mites are tiny round creatures that are barely visible, even when full-grown. They attack the underside of leaves and spin delicate webs. These mites are usually red but sometimes are orange, yellow or green. Usually a hand lens is necessary to detect them.

Red spider mites are well-adapted to living on plants in a home and thrive where the air is hot and dry. They are easily controlled if detected early. Spraying or dipping the plants in a solution of nicotine sulfate—1½ teaspoons of Black Leaf 40 dissolved in one gallon of warm water—is effective.

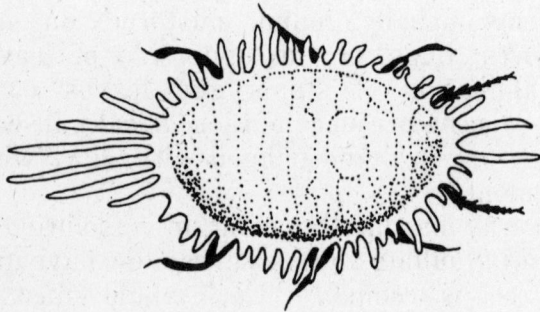

MEALY BUGS

Small cottony patches along leaf veins or at axils where stems join the main branch indicate mealy bugs. An additional symptom is a sticky secretion that forms shiny patches on the leaves. Mealy bugs are grayish white, oval shaped, and have numerous fringe-like filaments radiating in all directions. They are sucking insects that may be seen without a hand lens. An extremely large infestation of these insects causes stunting and death of the plant.

Mealy bugs can be removed with a stream of water or a brush. In serious cases, sprays of nicotine and white-oil-emulsion insecticides will control them. Malathion may also be used. Or swab off with alcohol-dipped cotton.

SCALES

Scale is a tiny insect that lives under an armor during its adult stage. Only when young can these insects move about.

Newly hatched scales are almost invisible. After inserting its proboscis (a tubular sucking organ) in a leaf or steam, a scale remains in one spot the rest of its life, sucking sap from the plant and growing larger. Mature scales are usually brown, while young ones are smaller, flatter and pale green.

Scale insects seriously reduce the vigor of infested plants. Foliage turns yellow and growth is reduced. Like aphids, they excrete a sticky substance that coats the foliage and encourages growth of a black fungus that resembles soot.

To clean a plant of scales, dip it in a diluted solution of nicotine sulfate. Sometimes it helps to dip a piece of cotton in either nicotine sulfate or alcohol and rub off the scales. You may also use house plant aerosol sprays. Washing house plants at regular intervals helps control scales.

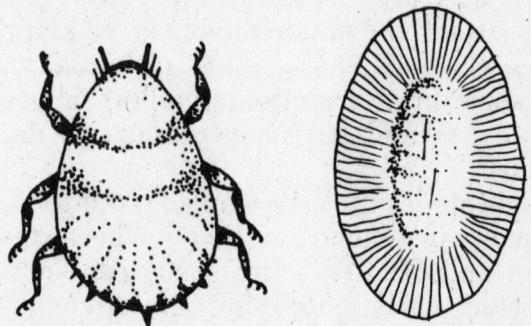

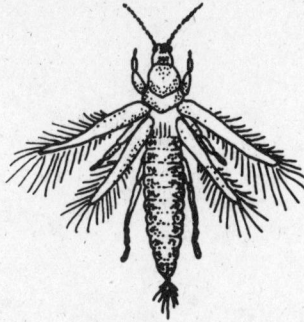

THRIPS

Thrips are brown or black creatures that live in crevices of small leaves around the growing point of a plant. A magnifying glass helps detect thrips. They are slender, pointed at both ends with bodies that lie close to the surface. Thrips have rasping mouthparts used to suck plant juices. The sucking of sap causes a streaky silvery appearance on the attacked foliage. Eventually leaves become brown and wilted and may drop from the plant. Thrips are easily eliminated by dipping or spraying with a nicotine insecticide as recommended for red spider mites.

CYCLAMEN MITES

Cyclamen mites are invisible to the naked eye. Since the African violet has become popular, cyclamen mites have become more prominent. Stunted, distorted leaves and flowers are symptoms of cyclamen mites. Sometimes they turn leaf margins up in cup shapes. On African violets they cause a hard, stunted center growth and a sickly light color.

Discard infected plants and observe strict sanitation to prevent spreading. A cutting should never be taken from a plant infested with cylamen mite because the new plant will certainly have mites.

NEMATODES

Plants troubled by nematodes have an unthrifty appearance, characterized by misshapen new leaves, bumps on leaves or stems, cessation of growth, and root knots. Discard affected plants; start over with fresh soil from nematode-free source.

Cleanliness is one of the most important factors in dealing with either diseases or insects. If it becomes necessary to cut away diseased portions of plants, always cut back to healthy growth. Keep your pruning tools sharp. A smooth, clean cut heals much more quickly. Disinfect all tools with denatured alcohol after pruning diesased parts of plants.

Treat wounds over one inch in diameter to prevent decay, disease, and penetration by insects while the wound is healing. The best wound dressing is asphalt varnish containing an antiseptic. An antiseptic prevents the spread of harmful organisms that may be present in the varnish. If you cannot get a dressing containing antiseptic, swab the wound with alcohol or coat it with shellac before varnishing. Apply the dressing as soon as the wound is dry. Asphalt varnish will not stick if the wound is wet.

If it becomes necessary to discard diseased plants, never put them in with composting material—burn or otherwise dispose of them. Disinfect the pots if they are to be used again, as well as the soil that will go into them.

GREENE